AF223619

# Jesus Loves Me
## This I Know

By

# Stephanie A. Stephens - Zellner

Published by Creation Publishing Group LLC
www.creationpublishing.com

© 2020 Stephanie A. Stephens Zellner
ISBN # 978-1-7366369-0-9
Library of Congress Number # 2021902441

All rights reserved. No part of this book may be used or reproduced, stored in, or introduced into, a retrieval system, or transmitted in any form or by any means without the express written consent of the publisher.

Published and printed in the United States of America.

Dedications to my family:

I love you all so much!
My twin brother Steve – for being SUPER
My sister-in-law Anna – for being ATTENTIVE
My sweet niece Sarah Grace – for having STAR Quality
My beloved son Hunter – for HUGE Accomplishments
My little sister Amy – for being Super AMBITIOUS
My big sister Renee – for being a RAZZLE Dazzler
My other sweet niece Jessica and Addy (her precious daughter) –
for being JOYFUL
My nephew Thibault – for being TURBO-Charged
My nephew Stewart – for being SATISFIED
And of course, my loving husband Michael – for being MINE!
Extended also to his sons and daughters and grandkids.
And finally, my mom, dad, and stepdad,
who are my guardian angels now.
And Dr. James (Jim) Jackson –
for being a truly nice friend and loving the Lord.
*"When your joy in me meets my joy in you,
there are fireworks of heavenly ecstasy"*
– from "Jesus Calling" by Sarah Young
Today, take note of the freedom and happiness
that is yours if you will only receive it.

# CONTENTS

# CHAPTER 1
## JESUS KNOWS

I REALLY KNOW AND believe that, so I thought it was a good title for my book. I know it from the Bible. It's not just basic instructions before leaving earth, it's the best instructions.

After that, though, I became an alcoholic at 14.

I know a big incident that happened to me caused me to start drinking so early in age…and that was my car accident.

I was born a twin sister to my brother 16 minutes later! My brother was sitting on my head and that started the brain damage. ☺ I have lots of twin jokes. I'm Stephanie Ann and my brother is Steven Dan. Isn't that special! He got the blue eyes and brains, and I got the green eyes and common sense (some of it anyway).

Steve is 6' tall and 200 lbs. I'm about 5'1" and 117lbs. Better than the other way around…hehehe! I told you I had twin jokes…

Anyway, he is my hero even though were complete opposites. He's like a big brother to me. He is very smart, and he took most of that, too. I was put back in fourth grade because I made an "F" in math. Am still not good at it, but it did help me being put back. I really had to struggle, always studying. I made A's, B's, and C's, so I did graduate but no top honors.

So I was a year behind my brother, and we weren't in touch so much. He excelled in football and was good-looking. The girls loved him. He got a football scholarship at TCU, but then tore ligaments in his knee and had to quit football. He finished college at the University of Houston.

I was in 8th grade and that's when my life changed forever.

# CHAPTER 2
## THE FALL OUT

I N 1972, MY parents went out for the evening, so I asked if I could walk down the block to my friend's house. They said ok but nowhere else. I agreed and left.

At my friend's Pam Cummings, we decided to get some friends from across the street and ride our bikes to another friend's house, Patricia, across town but not that far. I didn't have a bike, so I borrowed my neighbor Steve Sawyer's 10-speed…and it was dark.

The last thing I remember is waking up in the ER. I remember Pam was there, and I said, "I'm sorry." For what, I didn't know. My mom had a nervous breakdown and it wasn't looking good.

We were in Spring Branch, and our friends were ahead of me and Ronnie Strobel – he was good-looking! It happened at Gessner and Long Point. Supposedly, we were crossing the street, then a car hit me. I flew about 40 feet in the air and landed on the esplanade in between the streets (that and God saved my life).

I landed with my neck and head shifting to the side. Ronnie was there and said I tried to get up, but my leg and right wrist were broken. Then I went unconscious. The teenager who hit me was driving fast and drinking.

The way that I was thrown off the bike and landed tore the nerves from my spine and neck all down my arm and hand. The bone came out of my right wrist, and I had a compound fracture in my right leg. So it got my right side alright – real good.

In the ER at first, I didn't know what was wrong with me, but I couldn't move my right arm, it was paralyzed. It was pretty fuzzy for a while…I don't remember a lot.

The doctors fixed my wrist and leg, but couldn't do anything about my torn nerves. This was 1972.

Boy did my life change! I was in the hospital for a month. It happened on March 31st with the next day being April Fool's Day. Students at school didn't believe it because they thought it was an April Fool's joke. But it wasn't. As I said, it changed my life forever. It affected every person in my life seriously.

I did not and was not able to go back to school, so I had a homebound tutor come to our house.

I was so sad and depressed and thought God had punished me for lying to my parents. I should have listened to my mom and stepdad and just stayed at my friend's home. But you know how we don't always listen to our parents.

# CHAPTER 3
# MY UPBRINGING

L ET ME GIVE you a little background on my childhood. Born in Shawnee, Oklahoma, me, my twin brother, and my older sister Renee. My mother being single with three toddlers remarried my stepfather. He was a Jewish single man from New York, but he was in Oklahoma working at a store (like Target) as a merchandise manager. That's how they met. My mom was the receptionist. I don't remember a lot about that time, but they got married, and we moved to Houston, Texas – where I grew up.

Now I personally think God had a big part in this, and he works through people. My stepdad, Aaron Stehr, was head over heels for my mom. My mother didn't have a hard time saying yes to his proposal. God bless my stepdad. He's in heaven now. He had dementia.

We had a Christian mother and a Jewish stepfather, so we had mixed faiths in our household. I remember going to the synagogue and seeing an old man and started crying. I really don't know why.

Our childhood was bumpy and dysfunctional. My stepdad, whom I later called Daddy Aaron, yelled at us three kids a lot and grounded us a lot. in the beginning, it was just raising a family. My mom would take us to a Baptist church and we went to Sunday school. We really didn't go to the synagogue that much. But I remember every morning,

Daddy Aaron would put his little cap on and prayer shawl around his neck, and he would walk around and pray – maybe in Hebrew too – with this little Bible.

God bless Daddy Aaron.

The dysfunction was he never showed us affection or told us he loved us. But I believe he did it through raising three small children that weren't his and providing for us! And he didn't drink or smoke either.

Then, in 1965, my mom got pregnant! They had a little girl – Amy Lynn Stehr. I had a little sister! So now we four children were a family!

I had some things I was pretty self-conscious about. I had a pug nose and bow legs. And I was made fun of. I was very self-conscious about myself. Then, low and behold, I got a nose job, then my mom got one! I didn't have a pug nose anymore but was still bow-legged. But I was so happy about my nose!

I was 14 then and later had my car accident. I had a couple of boyfriends, but I didn't know anything about love. ☹

# CHAPTER 4
## TIME WILL MEND

From my car accident, I was in the hospital for a month. I don't remember a lot about that. I was angry with God and felt very shameful that I had disobeyed my parents and lied. I thought, "That's what I get for lying," and God was angry with me. And of course, "Why me? Why me?" I felt sorry for myself, too. I was in a wheelchair for a while, then got a walking cast. Boy, that was so much better! I went through a long period of rehabilitation. Mainly for my arm and hand. When I went home, I had a small stimulator machine. It had a padded round end on the handle and my mom, brother, or whoever, would place the padded end on certain muscle spots of my arm and hand (we had a paper instruction guide).

Anyway, when you pressed the little dial on the base, it would stimulate my muscle points. The higher you turned it, the more it hurt and you could see your skin jump. I think I was in shock without even realizing it. I don't remember my accident. Maybe that's a blessing in disguise! I just remember like in a dream, I was standing on a white curb and saw a car coming towards me. Thank God I'm alive! God and landing in the grass instead of the street, I believe God saved my life for a reason. Because I could be dead. The young man who hit me. I remember seeing him in court one time. I was just in shock. He didn't have any insurance. Wouldn't you know – I get hit by a car where the person has no insurance.

I got like $8,000 something when I should have gotten $80,000 – such is life.

But I'M ALIVE!

I remember my tutor was coming. I was real constipated, so much that my mom had to give me a suppository. I couldn't get up or move and ended up falling asleep on the bathroom floor. Needless to say, I went through a lot – tears, depression, shock, and more shock. It wasn't easy, but I'M ALIVE! Thank you Jesus for sparing my life!

Remember this happened in 8th grade. I was not able to go back to school for the rest of the year, but I do remember going to my 8th-grade dance with a dress on and in a wheelchair. I don't remember if I had a good time, but I went. And yes, I did graduate.

After I healed over the summer, I went into high school – Northbrook. I was so self-conscious of my arm to the extreme. Always wearing long sleeves even in the summer, even in the pool. I could not use my arm and didn't want anyone seeing it. At school, I put my purse on my lap to cover my arm and hand. Very self-conscious!

A prayer for mothers who have lost a precious child to a drunk driving accident or any other kind of accident. Amen.

# CHAPTER 5
## THE MONSTER

AFTER A WHILE, my right arm started to get skinny even though all of my physical therapy. So, I started wrapping it with two Ace bandages from my elbow down. It made me feel better, but now it was really noticeable. Even so, I wore them for a long time, probably making my arm skinnier. But I didn't care. Ironically, it made me feel better just covering up my arm.

In high school, I had friends but not that many. I was very shy and withdrawn. Carol Way was my best friend in the whole world. She lived close, so we hung out a lot together and we grew up. We grew up in Spring Shadows Subdivision and lived on the very last street of 12 blocks of homes. Actually, we had it made living on the last street - called Palo Pinto. Northbrook High School was built right behind the fence. First, it was an open pasture where a neighbor had a horse. But then they built the high school on the land and apartments were added later. Spring Shadows Elementary was around the corner on Kempwood, and Spring Oaks Jr. High was not far.

I was 14 years old and discovered alcohol. I would go to my friend Pam's apartment by Northbrook and her mom drank, so I started drinking too – mixed drinks! Well, that just invited me into the devil's den.

Suddenly, I was a different person – not shy, not so self-conscious, and had fun. So that started my drinking career days. I lost my virginity at 17 in the back seat at the drive-in movie theater. That drive-in theater was the thing back then. It was with Ronnie Strobel, my friend who was with me when the car accident happened. We were friends, then became a couple but eventually broke up. I was so drunk at the drive-in, I don't remember much except we had sex and there was blood.

# CHAPTER 6
## MY LIFE PATH

AFTER DISCOVERING ALCOHOL, I would go to our school dances. My friends and I would be out in the parking lot and drink beer before we went in. I was very self-conscious when I danced, but when alcohol was in me, it helped a lot (so I thought). I was more talkative and flirty, especially around friends and guys, which is what I wanted to be. I found a new perspective, new freedom. I loved it! So I thought....

*Father, please forgive me for lying and having the wrong ideas in my head, and being angry with you. In Jesus' name, amen.*

To me, my brother was a football star with a good brain. I was a drunk already having blackouts and going crazy. I remember climbing through Steve's bedroom window coming home late and drunk.

So started my world in the drinking business.

"Does anybody hear her, does anybody see her searching for hope? She yearns for affection that she never got at home." – Does Anyone Hear Her by Casting Crowns.

One time at my high school there was a terrible accident. A guy got hit on a motorcycle by a car right on the circular street that went around our school. It was awful! There was blood everywhere. I don't know what happened to that young man, but I prayed he wouldn't die. It reminded me of my car accident.

We had a four-bedroom house, and I'd say we were middle class. my older sister Renee and I shared a bedroom, Amy had a room, and Steve had a room with bunk beds. I remember I fell off the top bunk one time, but I was ok. We would fight over the fan. We both wanted the fan on us, so we fought as siblings do. One time, I came up and hit Renee in the back. She pulled the mattress off the bed to throw on me. Such are sisters!

I did have a life before my accident. I took ukulele lessons and played "Tip Toe Through the Tulips" by Tiny Tim (he sang and played the ukulele). Later, Renee and I took piano lessons. We had a little concert and got these trophy head busts of like Beethoven. I had that one.

# CHAPTER 7
## MY DEAR TWIN

I RAN TRACK IN junior high and liked running. When I was young, I pretended I was a horse (I love horses) and would run around. I had a stick pony. I loved it! I also had an imaginary friend always riding a horse. His name was Speedy. I would be riding home on the bus from Spring Oaks Jr. High and there would be Speedy riding alongside the bus, "Easy Rider."

Steve played football and was popular. Because of me being so self-conscious, feeling like a loner and black sheep of the family, mom favored Steve over me and I knew it. I just had to accept and live with it. But I love my brother Steve, my twin, dearly…he was like a big, older brother to me.

I didn't feel like I fit in anywhere.

Amy Lynn, my sweet little sister, was very smart and talented. She took dance for a few years. She was very good!

Renee was kind of a wild one, like me. She used to climb out the window of our one-story house and sneak out at night. On the other hand, I was coming home late and would come in through my brother's room window because I was so drunk.

I just drank during my high school days, then in my 20's started smoking marijuana. I like that, too, but drinking was my drug of choice and much easier to get.

By that time, my mom was going through depression. My sweet mother did have a job. When I was a senior and went half a day, my mom worked. I was in charge of preparing the meals. But in time, depression got the best of my mom, and my stepdad and she hardly talked. I think their marriage was falling apart. My mom should have been on an antidepressant, but she wasn't. My mom would spend the whole weekend in bed. One time I knocked on her door and asked if she wanted anything to eat, but she would always say no.

Flash forward twenty years – my mom got back with my real dad (after going to my cousin's wedding in Oklahoma). So, she ended up leaving my stepdad and remarrying my real dad! That was quite a shock for us all. My stepfather was heartbroken. I, Steve, and Renee had moved out, and Amy was there by herself with her real father. It was an unusual and dysfunctional situation. But we all survived –

My mom remarrying my dad was not a good situation. He was an alcoholic like me. I believe it's genetic. Some folks don't believe that, but I did and do now still. I got it, not my brother. This kinda defined us because I was a wild one with a drinking problem. Today, we're like complete opposites. Steve is more optimistic and I'm more pessimistic (my bipolar). He did his wildness in school but kept upgrades and got a scholarship at TCU for football. So he went. Then he tore the ligaments in his knee, had to quit football, and decided to come back to Houston. He finished school and graduated from the University of Houston.

I'm so proud of my brother because he lived at home in not so favorable conditions with our stepfather. He had a job at the Garden Shop at SAGE, the store where my stepfather was a merchandises manager. He paid his way through the rest of college himself, got into the banking business, and has been in it to this day. He's the president of a bank. I guess I talk a lot about my brother because he helped me out so much financially through the years.

Kudos to my big brother and twin brother, Steven Dan!

# CHAPTER 8
# ON THE BRAIN

I HAVE AN ADDICTIVE personality, so the darkness of alcohol entered my body and slowly poisoned me over the years. Then I became suicidal – the depression enveloped me like a blanket. In my 20's, I was diagnosed with depression/bipolar.

After high school, I got my first job at TRC (Texas Rehabilitation Commission) as their receptionist. They taught me how to type with one hand on a regular typewriter. I didn't want to learn on a special typewriter for one-handed people. I didn't want to be restricted to a certain type. So, I learned and I got to where I could type up to 40 words per minute – with one hand. My home keys were F, G, H, J, and went from there, all over that typewriter. Now it's considered a relic from the past. I'm kinda old school still in my later life. I'm very allergic to technology! It just confuses me and is very frustrating! So my career started with receptionist jobs. Back then, you didn't have to know the computer as much.

I tried all kinds of jobs just to see what I could do…like a waitress at Waffle House, which didn't last long. I just couldn't get all the orders on the table fast enough. Then I did sales, timeshare, Avon, telemarketing, which I really didn't like (I couldn't handle rejection very well and I was so sensitive). I didn't really go to college except taking an

English class, which I did very well. English and Art were my favorite subjects. And I took Spanish again even though I took it in high school. But I still couldn't get it.

Everybody moved out of the house as soon as they could. Renee moved in with a boyfriend. I moved in with a female roommate, finally out on my own. I don't remember the exact age, but I had freedom so I thought – I don't remember a lot about my childhood. I just don't remember very well. Renee or Steve would say, "Don't you remember this or that happening?". Sometimes it came to me as they talked about it or else it was just vague. I think my twin brother sat on my head too long!

I really thought I had brain damage early on because I struggled in school to make decent grades, had a bad memory, was bi-polar, then became an alcoholic early on. Then started smoking cigarettes in my 20's. You couldn't be in a club and not drink and smoke. It went hand-in-hand for me.

CHAPTER 9

# Funky Town

IN THE '80s, oh boy was disco in. I graduated in 1977 at 18, and Jessica my niece was born. We were the first graduating class to go all four years after Northbrook was built. It was nice and new! And not all the shooting and terrible things that go on today. I can understand how a person can just lose it ("snap" as some call it) and do violent things. Revenge is the way of the world and lack of forgiveness runs rapidly.

*Lord, help us to have world peace, and please use me as a bridge to link all people I meet to the acknowledgment of the Holy Spirit. Please forgive us, Lord, and help us. Then empowered by the Holy Spirit, we can rise above life's difficulties, strengthened to meet life's demands.* I believe the signs of the times are here, and we have to beware.

My first DWI was on S. Padre Island selling flowers in clubs. Obviously, I was probably driving crazy. I was put on probation for I think a year or two. How I got to S. Padre is a story in itself.

I was in a treatment center in Houston, which was converted from an apartment complex. I'm not sure how long I was there. I jogged then, so I'd have someone tie my bandana around my head and take off running the sidewalks inside the complex. There were quite a few gay women there, and I kinda made friends with this one girl. She came to me and was really friendly. I had gay friends before, so it was nothing new. When I worked at J. Christopher's Hair Salon for five years, most of the guys were gay, as was the boss. So, we were friendly towards each other. I believe in the Bible that being gay is wrong, but God says love on another, so I loved. I had female gay friends, but I was not gay and made it clear to them.

Anyway, at this treatment complex, they had a pool and hair salon. My hair was short and I bleached it there, and remember just sitting by the pool soaking in the rays until my time was up for my hair. It came out really blonde. Like Olivia Newton-John, that was the fad at the time – short hair and bandanas!

So I thought it was a pretty cool place. Until I found myself smoking a joint with some other girls around a table by the pool. There was no one around, but we were on the lookout so we wouldn't get caught. And we didn't. Boy, that was a trip. You can get drugs at a treatment facility!

To make things even worse, another time someone gave me a hit of acid and I took it. I was lonely and depressed, and so was my gay friend. So one night, we had a fling. I didn't do anything to her, but she did some things to me. I think she had a crush on me all this time and she was so nice and sweet. *God, please forgive me!*

This happened at night. The next morning, someone saw us or told the faculty and we were kicked out. What was I to do? *Please help me, Lord my God.* Was I a lesbian now?? I was sick to my stomach.

They sent us to another location. Another facility not far down the road. We were able to spend the night. They had been told we were lesbians, so we couldn't sleep in the same room. I said, "It's not true. She is, but I'm not." No one believed me.

So, my gay friend (Susan was her name) came up with some money, and we ran way to Corpus Christi in my car. Susan used to live there, so we drove there. I didn't know what world I was in – a real or fake one!

# CHAPTER 10
# S. PADRE

WE GET TO Corpus Christi, drinking all the way, and was running out of cash. So we thought of how we can make some money. In my frenzy drunken stupor, I went to bed with a guy for money. Oh, so now I'm becoming a prostitute?! I wanted to kill myself. The next day, Susan stole my clothes, which didn't fit her anyway, and my money. I was really stuck in an ugly situation. But the good Lord was watching over me, and I was rescued by my ex-broth-er-in-law. Renee's first husband, Bruce Larson. I called him "Brucey." *God, forgive me and save my soul!!*

I had to put my pen down and walk away for a long while writing about this story. It's painful and shameful.

My sister Renee told me Bruce was in Brownsville, so I contacted him and he came to get me. I was in Corpus all alone after Susan stole my clothes and money. I had my car, thank goodness. I was so glad to see Brucey. He was so kind, sweet, and would do anything for you. God was watching over me. So, we drove to S. Padre Island – me following him over the big bridge. I remember it took me two hours to drive over that bridge during Spring Break one time, and it was only about a mile long! Brucey was a mountain man. He loved the outdoors and the mountains. No wonder, Brucey was an Eagle Scout. This was in the middle 1990s and I lived there for a year. It a terrible year all around. I got this job back over the bridge before you enter S. Padre at Eddie's BBQ restaurant. This girl and I who worked there became friends. We would pop diet pills to give us crazy energy. It kinda made me sick, but my friend was like eating them. I'm not sure how short a time I worked there because I was drinking. When you're young and drinking, it seems like you could do a lot of things. But that's also when I sold flowers in clubs and got my first DWI. I was a drinker and so was Brucey. He always had a small glass that had vodka in it; all the time, he drank vodka straight.

My dear Brucey is in heaven now. He died from alcohol-related complications. Rest in peace, my dear sweet Brucey.

God saved me and now I was living (me and Brucey) in a three-story house. He rented us two separate rooms. It was a really cool house.

Now some things are fuzzy to me while I lived there because of all the drinking and drugging. Did I say drugs, too – oh yes. At a gym I was going to, I meet George doing karate. We meet and become friends, then kinda boyfriend/girlfriend, so I thought. He was the "candy man" on the island selling cocaine to all who wanted to buy. We became close and ended up moving into a duplex together, so I got it free! We had separate bedrooms, which turned out to be a good thing.

He had girls coming over a lot for "candy." They'd go in his room and be in there for a while. So either he was having sex or getting blow jobs for the girls to get free cocaine. I got real depressed. I was drinking a lot and eating a lot after I drank, so I popped up to almost 130 lbs. Too much for petite me. On top of that, one of the times I was too drunk and stupid, I entered a homemade bikini contest. George wrapped my private parts and boobs with saran wrap and glitter in the tub. I was so nervous, depressed, and self-conscious – I don't know why I did it. I was crazy and stupid. I wanted to win the $500 prize money. But my friend Amy, who lived on a boat with her boyfriend, won. She was beautiful with long blonde hair and a great body. She made her bikini out of seashells with a lot of skin showing. She was beautiful! I knew I wasn't winning. I was happy for her, but kinda jealous because I had gained all this weight. We still stayed friends. There were other times in my life when I drank and didn't eat…I weighed 100 lbs.! Alcohol does put weight on you, especially beer.

But on Padre Island (of all places), I was miserable, fat, and depressed.

# CHAPTER 11
## FRAGMENTED PIECES

WE HAD SOME good times, too. We had a party one time (well, George did) and a couple we knew did sand sculptures on the beach. We didn't live but just across the road and then there was the beach. Anyway, they made this sculpture out in our front yard to show where the party was. It was pretty cool!

But there were few good times because I drank and drugged the whole time I lived there – a year.

All that time, I was so depressed and I really didn't have a love relationship with George the candy man. I'm kinda glad I didn't. No telling what STD I could have gotten from him. I think he got around with girls making all those deliveries of cocaine.

I started having suicidal thoughts of jumping off this tall building across the street. I chickened out, but I did hurt myself. I was sitting on the banister of our two-story duplex and just let go and fell right over the top. I fell on my back and in an ant bed. George came up to me and asked if I needed help. I was so mad at him, I said no. I barely got up, but I managed. I hurt my back and couldn't see a doctor because I had no money and wasn't working then. That was my second suicide attempt. I had to stay in bed for a while because my back hurt so much

– and, as I mentioned earlier, my first DWI selling flower in clubs. So now you know why that was not a good year for me.

Brucey was still around, but we didn't see much of each other by then.

God bless his heart for saving me from a disastrous situation. May he rest in peace. He was the nicest guy ever!

I don't recall how I got back to Houston. I blacked out a lot during my drinking days, so a lot is fuzzy to me.

There was a lot about my childhood I don't remember either so my brain injuries started early. Always had a hard time remembering things. I told you my brother was sitting on my head. ☺ Just another joke, but I started to believe it!

My first suicide attempt was when I was living with my brother in his townhouse. I was drinking and hiding my bottles of Thunderbird. I drank the cheap bottles of wine or Mad Dog 2020. Anyway, I had a bottle under the kitchen cabinet and up in my bedroom closet. I drank and maintained. I got a job selling timeshares at Seven Coves in Conroe, TX. I made a big sale and remember buying my mom's car. That job didn't last long because all they did was party and drink. I fit in…but I didn't. Does that make sense? The drinking got too much, and I couldn't do my job anymore. Most of my jobs didn't last long.

I was drinking, single, lonely, and depressed. So I decided to take all the pills in my bottle of anti-depressants and die. I called my brother and told him I loved him. I went to sleep not expecting to wake up, but I did. It didn't work! Another time while I was still living with Steve, I swallowed a whole bunch of black mollies but just threw up and got sick to my stomach. I didn't die then either. I guess I wasn't taking the right pills. *Lord, if I kill myself, will I still go to Heaven? If I repent and ask forgiveness, will you take me up there with you?* I didn't know and wasn't sure, so I decided to postpone it. I was blessed and the good Lord was watching over me. He protected me and I was honored.

Back on the Island….

There was this girl who Brucey introduced me to on S. Padre. She was a very good artist and painted a toucan at the beach on a big flat rock. It's beautiful and I have it to this day on my patio. She was living in an empty bus on the outskirts at the end of the Island. She would get naked, sit atop her bus and just chew peyote and mushrooms. I joined her but didn't get naked. Such was my life on S. Padre. A wasted lonely life. I don't remember how I got off the Island and made it back to Houston, but I did after living there a year. A year mainly of loneliness and depression and disgust, and I haven't been back since.

# CHAPTER 12
# THE MEAN GREEN

MY FIRST HUSBAND was Mickey G., and I met him out by the swimming pool sunbathing in a bikini and long-sleeved shirt. I was so hot but was too self-conscious to dress any other way. I had a female roommate, but we later split ways. We just didn't get along. I had put an ad in the Greensheet for a roommate. The ad said, "Looking for a fun-loving roommate to share a two-bedroom." I got some strange calls. I should have not put that in my ad.

So, I meet Mickey and his hangout crew by the pool. He came over to me and started flirting. That's about all it took for me to get involved with him. I was so lonely!! But what a BIG mistake it was. A dangerous mistake. In the beginning, it was good – he was a big cowboy-kinda guy with a mustache, beard, and cowboy hat. He always wore it. And drank (a lot) and smoked. I thought we were two lost souls put together by the devil himself. Anyway, he was good to me in the beginning. But he was kind of forceful and loud, and always had his crew of fellow druggies with him. We did not do drugs, just drank and smoked. And drank we did. I didn't have to pay for the alcohol – Mickey had it. I was in my early 20's. I thought I had it pretty good. I liked him a lot, though he was good-looking and because he was a big guy. I felt protected by him and safe. But boy, was I dead wrong! He did swimming pool work but was always drinking. He didn't seem to work that much – but he had money. One thing I really didn't care for was hanging out at the topless bars. Then, I found myself working in one as a waitress, not a dancer. They wanted me to dance, but I was too self-conscious of my arm. I thought for sure I 'd do it if I got drunk, but it didn't happen. *Thank you, Jesus!*

Mickey would come where I was working and start trouble because he was the jealous type. Should have been a big red flag, but it made me feel kinda good in a way. It made me feel attractive that he was jealous, and he said my arm didn't bother him.

But only a few weeks of knowing him, we were in the parking lot of a topless bar and had some kind of disagreement. The next thing I knew, he pulled his arm back and slapped me hard in the face. Wow, that hurt! I was shocked! I thought he would protect me not hit me. I started crying. We got in his car and left to some friend's house. By that time, I had a swollen black eye. He just kept drinking and partying, finally passing out. I just cried and cried. And no one seemed to care. This one girl told me to get Preparation-H for my eye. It would reduce the swelling. The next day, he was like nothing ever happened – second red flag. Would I run, walk away and leave him? No, I did not…and stayed with him for four years. Things got better, then there would be more abuse. In the bed, he was forceful with sex – the third red flag. But I still stayed and still we both drank. One time, I was naked and he started hitting on me and pushing me around. I don't even remember why. Then he pushed me. I fell on the closet floor and he was kicking me. I don't even know what he was saying. I was probably in a blackout. I remember my older sister Renee and her boyfriend came over (by that time, we were living together). I was in bed still naked. They wanted me to leave with them, but I didn't. So why did I stay? For more alcohol, drugs, and/or abuse? I don't know. I was crazy – I thought I loved him and he really did love me. A sick kind of love. That night, I had a black eye and prayed to God to help me. But, I wasn't helping myself.

Then one day, Mickey came home with a gun (a .357 magnum).

He did a drug deal with his gang of friends. It went bad…the drug dealer got shot and died.

So, the next thing I know, Mickey is going to prison with some of his friends. I was scared and wondered how the hell I got myself into this mess. But I was young, stupid, and immature and though I still loved him. I visited him and we wrote letters to each other. He would tell me how sorry he was that he hurt me and how much he loved me. Then he told me if I married him, he would get out earlier. So, I said ok, but I had to get someone to stand in for him (through proxy) because they would not let him out to stand by me at the courthouse.

I asked Carol, my best friend in the whole wide world, and she did it. I don't think she really wanted to do it, but I know she did it for me.

Mickey did get out early after about twelve months. He changed good and looked good – lost weight, lifting weights, and stuff like that. I thought a new, changed man – I'm in love! But it wasn't love. I didn't want to be alone. Like most everybody, right?! Thankfully, I had no children because I wouldn't want them to get hurt or go to CPS because I was a drunk.

After a few months, Mickey started getting real paranoid about the murder of the drug dealer. Mickey didn't shoot him, but he thought his friends were out for revenge against him. So, he started toting the gun around. I didn't feel so safe anymore.

*Dear Lord God, please protect me! Amen.*

We later rented a house. I would cook and stuff. We had thrift store furniture, and I tried to make it a home. We got in a fight one night, and he pointed the .357 magnum at me. I was sitting on the couch scared. He pulled the trigger and the bullet whizzed through the air, went by my hip and into the couch then to the floor. I freaked out, but I still stayed with him. We moved again, things got worse. I had to get out. Mickey was really paranoid. I called my real dad (this was when my mom and dad were back together). I asked him to come get me. I was leaving Mickey. He kept pointing the gun at me. My dad took a long time. The reason being – he brought the police. Mickey was getting really freaky and acting crazy. I was afraid. When was my dad coming?? I told Mickey I was going to my parents, who lived in Conroe, TX at the time.

When they came, the police pulled out their guns because Mickey was pointing the gun right at them. They told him to get down on the floor. They put him in handcuffs. I thought Mickey was my man, but seeing him handcuffed and laying on the floor put a different taste in my mouth, one of disgust. So Mickey went to jail and I was safe. My dad drove me to Conroe to stay with them. After four years of craziness, I finally got out. *Thank you so much, my sweet Jesus!* And for the police.

# CHAPTER 13
# THE END

I THOUGHT IT WAS all over, but not quite. A couple of months later, two detectives came to my mom and dad's home asking me questions about Mickey because he was dead; got shot in the neck over another woman. They had all the letters I'd written him in prison and wanted to know if I wanted them. They also wanted to know if I knew anything about his death, which I didn't. Supposedly, he got in a fight at his apartment with a neighbor over a girl. I think he was probably abusive to her, too. But he got mad, shot a bullet through the floor but it ricocheted and shot the woman in the leg. Then Mickey and this other man got in a fight. I imagine the neighbor was trying to protect the woman. So, he got shot in the neck and was slumped over sitting on a barrel. His door was left open, someone found him like that and called the police. That's what the detectives told me. But no one knows what really happened because they weren't there.

So that's my story about my first husband – the mean Green. I also believe in leaving vengeance to the Lord. One time, Mickey was in his car without me. We had a fight and somehow he shifted the car, backed up, and had his arm hanging out the window. He slammed his arm and hand into a steel beam and practically snatched off his hand. After that, it became deformed and he couldn't use it as well. It was the hand he hit me with at the topless bar years before. It was finally over. I was free but not from fear. Couldn't get away from the fear of this or that. Maybe Mickey put that fear in me. II Timothy 1:7 – *"For God did not give us a spirit of fear; but of power, love and a sound mind."* Why wouldn't that sink into my thoughts, in my brain? I don't know. I needed to work on that!

Something I forgot to mention about my marriage to Mickey G. When I was divorcing him, I found out he was still married to his first wife. So it was annulled. As I had mentioned earlier, he was a pretty jealous person. Once, I was walking home from the store. When I got home, he accused me of being with another man. We were both drinking. And when I was drinking, I would fight back. We were fighting and I came towards him – more like I lunged at him. When I did, he stuck his fist out and hit me in the mouth knocking out my nearly perfect two front teeth. One was cracked in half and the other was gone. It had to be with a great force. I thought he was going to knock me out. I was so angry. I shouldn't have lunged at him. That happened after we had recently met. Why was I not paying attention to ALL the red flags?! We got my teeth fixed, somehow, and I had caps put on. And I stayed with him.

I didn't want to be alone and didn't have any money. In a way, I loved him, but I knew it wasn't the true meaning of love like in the Bible. I Corinthians 13:4 – *"Love is the greatest!"* Read it sometime. It's like an impossible demand. But that's true love. Mickey said no one would love me because of my arm.

# CHAPTER 14
# MY CAREERS AND DETOX

I WORKED TRYING ALL different jobs to see what I could and could not do because of my arm. After graduating, my first job was for TRC (Texas Rehabilitation Center). I was their receptionist, and they taught me how to type with one hand (up to 40 words a minute). But I can't type like that anymore. So, I did receptionist jobs for a while. I signed up with two or three temp agencies, and they kept me busy. I worked and drank and maintained for a long time. Through all that, I was going in and out of treatment centers trying to get sober. Sometimes I would stay sober a few months, or a month and other times go buy alcohol as soon as I left the facility.

My brother Steve would pay for the ones that weren't free. I am so indebted to him – he's done so much for me through my entire adult life. I think the best way to pay him back was to stay sober, but I couldn't stay sober. I went to Cenikor and was there for a few months. But they were strict and weird, and I didn't like being there. I got so upset at a meeting that I threw my chair on the floor. I was ready to leave.

Then I went to a detox center called "Way Out Women's Detox" in Pasadena, TX. After a couple of months, they made me the assistant manager. New girls came in all the time. It was good and bad there. The good time was in the morning before we opened (we had AA meetings there). We'd all do our chores, and I would play my Russ TaffCD on my boom box. I would play my favorite song and sing along with him in the microphone. It was Christian music and I think God saved this girl there who was digging the song, too. When she left, she asked me for the title of the CD and said she was going to buy it. Maybe, just maybe, God helped her working through me to maybe save her soul. I could only pray for her. I hope she made it in life.

I had one bad experience there. A crude sexual comment made by a man about my body. Sometimes, I thought AA meetings were like meat markets – meaning the men hitting on the women, making comments. As if it was a requirement for the men to harass the women to come to AA.

Well, I met this guy there. I don't remember his name, so I'll call him "Kevin." I'm no angel, and we started flirting with each other. He started coming around every day. When my time was up there at the facility (it was mainly a detox center), I moved in with Kevin. He lived with his brother and his girlfriend in a run-down mobile home. Soon as we left the detox center, we drove to the store to get some beer. I chose Mad Dog 2020. I would drink a whole bottle (very stingy with my alcohol) and get pretty drunk. So in blackouts, I lived there for a while. I found a stray dog that was a part pit bull/part share pet and named him "Groucho." He was so pretty – black with a white chest and had wrinkles around his face and tale, but he looked like a pit bull. I would walk to the store with him and people would go to the other side of the road. He growled at me sometimes, hence the name Groucho. Then I found a stray kitten in our tree because the dogs were barking at him. I got him down and named him "Runaway." Now I had a kitten, too. I love animals!

Kevin and I parted ways and I went to live with my parents again. I brought Runaway, but my dad said he had to stay with his friends, who had dogs. One of the dogs bit Runaway's tail in half. He ran into the woods and never came back.

CHAPTER 15

# LIVING IN CONROE, TX

LIVING IN CONROE with my parents was a challenge. They were already having problems because my dad was drinking and my mom was really depressed. And I was drinking too; my dad and I would go out and drink together. Bad combination! We drove my mom crazy and that wasn't the worst of it. *God forgive me!*

I started going to bars to drink. One time my dad showed up. He was driving around Conroe looking for my car. I'm a grown woman and my dad told me to go home, but I didn't. When I got home (rather late), my dad locked me out of the house. I had to sleep in my car. When he drank a lot, he got mean and talked about negative things; seeking revenge against people he thought had done him wrong. One time, he hit my mom in the face with the phone. Another time, he tried to choke me and my mom pulled him off. If my mom had not done that, I don't know what would have happened.

There were times and some months that my real dad didn't drink. He was the nicest guy. But when he drank, he was very unpredictable.

My mom's life was like that after she remarried my real dad. Her life was a mess and, I'm sure, afraid at times. They built their beautiful house in Conroe (two bedrooms and a loft upstairs). But they eventually sold it and moved to Tomball, TX; built a small one-bedroom house there. My dad could do just about anything and loved tinkering with the car. So it was a turbulent relationship, especially for my mom. Maybe she thought she should have stayed with Aaron my stepdad, but she didn't love him. And that's a big deal. We had all moved away from home, and when my mom left, it was just Amy and my stepdad (her real father).

As I've said, I have a bad memory and just don't remember a lot. in my drinking times, I had a lot of blackouts. I drove in blackouts with three DWI's to show for it, and a PI (Public Intoxication) outside a club. Disco was in then, and I was clubbing a lot. I got free drinks after a little flirting, so I did good (so I thought). Even went home with a few. Sometimes when I awoke the next morning, I didn't remember anything! That's sad. So, to get over the depression, I would drink in the morning to numb myself. I didn't want to feel or face anything. I was so lonely! With three DWI's, I should have gone to prison, but one fell through the cracks. I really think God had something to do with that.

# CHAPTER 16
# JAIL TIME

WHEN I DROVE on the wrong side of the freeway, I got stopped. Thankfully! I could have killed innocent people. I think I would kill myself. I wouldn't be able to take it. Anyway, I went to jail (not my first time). All I can remember is bright white lights in front of me. I got on the exit ramp onto the freeway. It's just a miracle I didn't hit anyone. The policeman put handcuffs on me in the front because of my arm, but the handcuff fell off my right wrist. They were too big or my arm was too skinny. Probably the latter, I'm pretty sure. I went to the Harris County jail. I called Steve so he would know where I was. He said he would come bail me out. But I'll never forget what I told him, "I did this to myself and I deserved it." So, I was staying. It was miserable. I was there a week. I crawled into my sleeping area and slept as much as I could. Had to shower out in the open with male police walking by. I'm really quite modest when I'm sober. I was supposed to go to the mental health ward in the jail because I'm bi-polar, and they were supposed to give me medicine, but neither happened. I only had what they gave us to wear and you couldn't wash, so I hand washed my socks. They never did dry out before I left. When my horrible week was over, we were in line and this policewoman was checking ID bracelets. I had my damp socks in my hand and when

I raised my arm to show her my bracelet, she stopped my hand and said, "I don't want your dirty stinking socks." I was trying to tell her I washed them, but that didn't matter. We were shoved along like cattle. Steve came and picked me up. It was nice to be out in the sunshine. *Father, please forgive me – I know not what I do.* I don't remember where I went after Steve picked me up. Probably another treatment center.

# CHAPTER 17
# AUSTIN, TX

⸻⊰◆⊱⸻

I'M ON A bus to Austin to go to Rusk, a detox treatment center. Supposed to be highly recommended. I was very restless and didn't want to be there. I remember we were eating a plate of sausage. Then I just went nuts, picked my plate up, and threw it against the wall. The sausage reminded me of a man's penis, and I hated men. Mickey put a bad taste in my mouth about men. I was at Rusk for two to three days. I couldn't stand it. I knew I wasn't through drinking, SO I LEFT. Then I was stranded in Austin, TX. *Lord, forgive me for I know not what I do.* I didn't call Steve either to bail me out again or come to my rescue, because I knew God was my rescue.

I ended up walking down 6th street and met this guy with a hook arm selling flowers from a cart. We become acquainted. I asked him if I could sell flowers, too, and he said yes. He lived or rather stayed above an antique store run by two gay guys. It had a mattress and that was about it. This was a time when I hardly ate anything and weighed about 100 lbs. So, he set me up a cart on a corner of 6th Street – the party and clubbing scene. Well, I was doing pretty good. I met this little black guy that could sing like Johnny Mathis. We became friends and he'd sing to me. I loved it.

But not all was well – I was at my cart one night and my hook arm friend brought me a bottle of Thunderbird, per my request. I told you I was a cheap wino. I drank the whole bottle and passed out at my cart. Low and behold, like out of nowhere, my hook arm friend was there. I awoke remembering that he helped me. He took me to his place and I crashed on his mattress. He was very nice and respectful, didn't try anything on me.

Then he was gone and I wake up with policemen shining their bright flashlights in my face. They said, "Get out!" I was hopeless. The lost and lonely people. Didn't see my hook arm friend again. But he saved me from danger. I believe God works through people, and he was my angel that night.

I hooked up with my other friend. I'll call him "Johnny" because he sang like Johnny Mathis. We became friends, and I stayed with him for a while. He had another friend, and the three of us just drank and partied. They were nice to me and didn't try to rape me. Speaking of rape – I've been there, too. How about four times that I do remember… maybe more in blackouts. It's one of the worst feelings a woman can go through. And rape to me is taking sex against your will!!

## CHAPTER 18
# BROKEN BUT NOT DEAD

I HAD MET THIS guy named Roger, who was a roofer. We became a couple and moved in together. We did pretty well for awhile. He made me a kitchen table like a picnic bench. I had a great bottle collection of different shaped alcohol bottles. One was a real tall wine bottle. I had an old-time payphone in the kitchen. It was just for looks. We had a party by the pool, and I made most of the food. We had a good time. The only thing though, we both drank. After a while, Roger would go to work and stay gone all day. I had a feeling he was messing with other women. Well, I was no saint, and I partied with my neighbors. I was with some guy friends, I had a blackout. I don't really remember, but I know something happened because my body felt violated. I thought Roger was fooling around on me, so I did the same to get back at him. But I didn't like the feeling it gave me. Sick to my stomach.

Roger wanted sex one night, but I didn't. I struggled and he put his hand over my mouth and nose. When I tried to scream, he put his fingers in my eyeballs. I thought he was going to poke my eyes out! That was it. It was over between me and Roger. I was afraid but was not going to stay in another abusive relationship.

We broke up, and I went to stay with my older sister Renee. She was married to Brucey then. Roger and I talked because we had stuff in storage together. One day, he wanted to come by and go to the storage unit. So I let him in my sister's house thinking all was ok. Renee, Brucey, and their daughter Jessica (born the year I graduated, in 1977) were at a friend's house swimming. I thought everything was ok, but when I walked to my room, Roger grabbed me from behind and literally ripped my shorts off, threw me on the bed and had his way with me. I was shocked and hurt that he would rape me at my sister's. But he did. He got his stuff out of storage and that was the end of us!

My relationships were not healthy because both my partner and I drank and/or drugged. It was poisoning me. I was too stupid to see the portrait I was painting of myself. And it was dangerous. *Dear God, help me want to quit and forgive my sins. Amen.*

Another rape happened at a high school party. Another when I was drunk and hitchhiking. A pleasant man said he'd give me a ride, but first, he had to go to his apartment. Well, you can guess what happened. I'm surprised I don't have AIDS. Thank God! I've been tested more than once.

My high school friend Stephanie B. died of aids. She got it from her husband who fooled around on her. So very sad. I hung out with her for a while. She always had friends over drinking, smoking marijuana, and just hanging out. We'd take pills and get high. Stephanie B. forbade me to drink around her because she knew I was an alcoholic. So I didn't, or else I'd come over when I'd already been drinking. But she would get so mad at me. *Rest in peace, my dear friend.* She borrowed my car one night and had a wreck – totaled it out. That's the break. It is what it is.

# CHAPTER 19

# Pure Crazy

I DID HITCHHIKE SOMETIMES, one time on the freeway! I was involved with Tim (met him through AA). I went back drinking and he stayed sober. Probably still is. He was a nice guy, but I think he was in love with himself and his muscles. Anyway, I was drinking and walked on the freeway, started sticking my thumb out. A taxi picks me up. He didn't charge me. We went by a store and he bought a six-pack of beer. We drank it on the way. I was headed to Tim's apartment. When I got there (unexpectedly), Tim and I got in a big fight. I started trashing his plants. He got me out of there. I don't even know how I got home or which home I had.

When I was hanging out with gay friends, I used to go to gay bars with them. I needed some money, so someone arranged for me to have sex with this man. Then I'd have money. So I did it in half of a blackout. I passed out. When I woke up, I was naked, the man was gone and no money. I was so mad and crazy then. I couldn't find my dress and needed help. So in my drunken stupor and craziness, I ran out of the motel room naked and started banging on doors for help. I didn't know how anybody was really going to help me. What? Find my dress? I banged on a couple of doors, but no one answered. I was naked, running around the second floor of the motel and no one was around. Not even security. I felt so alone. I went back to the room and finally found my dress. Got dressed and left not knowing where to go. *Lord God, I thank you for protecting me from harm.* If security or anyone saw me, they might have called the police seeing a crazy naked woman running around. I thought it was weird that no one saw me!

# CHAPTER 20
# WORKING AND DRINKING

IN MY JOBS, I started drinking at lunch, then in the mornings on the way to work. At J. Christopher's Hair Salon, there was a bar down the strip center. Me and my friend Pye, who cut my hair, would walk down there and drink a Long Island Iced Teas. Boy, I'd go back to work feeling fine! They also served wine to our customers. And sometimes, a couple of the guys and I worked with would go to the car and smoke some pot, too. It was the best and favorite job I had. I was involved with Mickey then. This was in the late 1980s.

I got another job at RCA in customer service. Mainly phone work, especially in the evenings. I worked with two black girls. I was friends with one, the other one hated me and that got me emotionally, really affecting me.

My boss was tall, dark, and handsome – and single. I got involved with him. What a mistake. We'd meet at clubs and go to his place to have sex. One time I started my period after we had sex and blood was running down my legs. How embarrassing! It was such a mess!

At work during lunch, I would go buy an Orange Julius and pour vodka in it (you can't smell it, right?!), go back and drink it while doing phone work. Boy, I felt fine and thought I was great on the phone. But it was just a cover-up of what I was feeling inside. A lot of stress! The black girl who hated me really bothered me. I wanted everyone to like me! But it doesn't usually happen like that in life. Not everyone is going to like you.

My drinking went on for a while until I would get drunk at work. And in the mornings on my way to work, I'd drink straight vodka to calm my nerves. I was miserable, I thought beyond repair. But God was watching over me.

After a while, it got really bad. I was drunk or the effects of it in my system were evident at work. But my insurance I had through RCA paid for me to go into treatment. So I went. I made such an ass out of myself, I could never go back.

It took a long while for me to get over my anger toward God for my car accident. I wasn't angry, I was misguided. Because God did not punish me, he saved my life – I didn't die! He protected me again. I didn't lose my life. What a miracle! I really believe landing on the grass esplanade instead of the street saved my life. *He loves me and nothing can separate me from His love for me.*

It caused me unknowingly to be the person I am today. It caused me to step into dangerous situations that otherwise could have been deadly. Each time I was in a bad situation, God got me out of it. Through my drinking days, I often prayed to God to help me and He did. There are consequences to every sin, I sure had my share. But God did help me. I look back years later…I couldn't see how many endless times he saved me, but he did. There's a reason I had my accident; I don't know why, but sometimes I would sense the reason for it. But not entirely. God saved me from death many times and protected me even in the really bad times.

# CHAPTER 21
# BLINDED

---

I WAS DIAGNOSED WITH bipolar depression in my late 20's. I always wondered why I was so ignorant, slow, and had a hard time remembering things. And of course, depression. They put me on meds that I take to this day. But when I drank, I usually wouldn't take them. I heard you could get really sick or die mixing the two. So, I just didn't take them. And alcohol is a depressant. No wonder. No wonder – I knew God forgave me, but it was hard forgiving myself because I knew it was wrong and that's not how God does it. *He first loves and forgives us and He wants us to do for others the same.* People got put in my life along the way and God used me to help others even in my bad situations. But I just couldn't see it then. I was blinded by alcohol and drugs. I did my fair share of drugs – pot, cocaine, LSD, and ecstasy pills, but never did heroin. Thank God! My drug of choice was alcohol. It was too easy to get – I said I'd never shot up, but I did one time with cocaine.

CHAPTER 22
# HABIB K.

MY SECOND HUSBAND was Habib K., who was Arabic. I married him so he could get his US Citizenship card. I met him through my best friend, Carol. He was a bartender at private parties and was going to the University of Houston. Very nice guy. We had to live together to know things about each other for some test. He paid me a fair amount that basically paid my car payments. We did not have the spark in our relationship. That would have been nice since we legally got married in a courthouse. If we could have for real fell in love, it would have made it easier. But I wasn't attracted to him in any way sexually. So, it was a business contract with him. I was sober when we got together, but after a few months, I started drinking again. He would get upset when I drank at home and then go out. He said, "Please stay at home if you're going to drink." But I would get antsy and wanted to go party. I tell you it was a miracle that God protected me (and others) from not wrecking my car, all the times I drove while drinking!

Once, I went on a train ride to Los Angeles to meet Habib. I just remember meeting him up there to drive back with him for company. The train ride was awesome! But haven't been on one since. I got to sightsee a little bit – the Chinese Theater, the stars' Stars engraved in cement. It was pretty cool.

We stayed married for two years and faithful to the contract. My husband Habib got his citizenship! And we both went on with our lives.

# CHAPTER 23
# STUPID ME

ONE TIME I stopped at a store to get two tallboy beers. I ran in but to my mistake (a stupid one), I left my car running. I came right out and there was this Mexican sitting in my car. I said, "Hey, what are you doing?" he looked up quickly and drove off with me running after him. I couldn't believe it! My car got hijacked! I called the police and reported it. A few days later, they found my car (not stripped), thank God! There were tools in the back seat, a full tank of gas, and a six-pack of beer in the front seat. I couldn't believe my eyes! So, I got my car back and drank that beer. Gave the tools to somebody....

Another adventure I had was hanging out at Stop 'N Go's asking people coming out of the store if they had any marijuana. I did some pretty bold things when I drank. I met this guy, Karl R. was his name, and he was an ex-Houston Oiler football player! He was very nice, got me some pot, and introduced me to crack. Now let me tell you, that is the nastiest drug ever. But I'm an addict, so I had to try some. It was a crazy, crazy experience. I remember one day I was driving my car and in the back seat, Karl R. and a friend were cooking and getting the crack ready. I just remember saying, "You better save me some." I did that for a while.

I met this other guy, don't remember his name. Doesn't matter. It was all drug-related. I went to a party and this man, who was older than me. I knew he anticipated having sex. But I just remember looking at this good-looking younger guy and ME wanting to have sex with him. Crack makes you do crazy things. It's like you get really horny. Thank God nothing happened with either guy. Got out of that situation and can't remember any more of it.

# CHAPTER 24
# THE IGUANAS

ANOTHER ADVENTURE WAS when I saw two iguanas outside sunning themselves in a motel room. I was really depressed and just driving by this motel, not knowing where to go. I saw this guy sitting out there with the iguanas and said, "Hi, I like your iguanas." We got to talking and that night I was partying with him. He was part of a demolition team from California doing some work in Houston. He, his crew, and I moved into another motel off of Telephone Road together. All we did was drink and smoke. We had so my empty beer cans in our room, it looked like we had a major party.

I remember me and this guy were drinking hard liquor, and we got in a fight. He took the liquor bottle and hit me in the head. That hurt!

Then my brother and dad drove over to where I was to check on me. I had called them and told them where I was (not that I wanted to see them). I had a habit of not calling my family when I was drinking. I was embarrassed and depressed and ashamed, but I didn't go with them. I stayed in that dirty motel with those guys. I was only involved with that one guy.

I was previously staying with a couple who would let girls stay with them who didn't have any place to go at the time. They were from the Way Out Women's Detox Center – it was a while back. Don was the man's name and he had like 30 years of sobriety. His wife drank but he didn't. I remember she had a crush on my boyfriend Tom when he would come over. I was sober then. But that lasted only a few months. When I went back out, shortly after that, I saw the iguanas and that guy. Tim and I had broken up. He stayed sober. How come I couldn't? A few months, maybe a year, but then I'd go back out again. I was running around in circles and getting the same result.

Throughout my life, I prayed for God to help me stop. I grew up in church and believed in God.

Sometimes I was just so lonely or felt like a loner, even with a boyfriend. There was that void in my soul again. I know now, but not back then, that Jesus was by my side through it all the whole time. I guess I wasn't reaching out far enough. So I thought. I didn't really know Jesus. I knew of him.

Another guy I lived with bashed my head against the kitchen because I wouldn't give him a blow job. I was living in Conroe where my parents lived. I remember my mama and granddad were in town from Oklahoma. I was supposed to go visit them. I was talking to my mama with tears streaming down my cheeks – I had a swollen face and black eye from the kitchen floor, so I couldn't go visit. And I couldn't tell her why....

# CHAPTER 25
# MY ANGEL BOY

WHEN I WAS 42 years old (in 2000), I got pregnant! And didn't even know I was.

I met Donald White from AA, and we started a friendship. I was sober at the time. Hallelujah! He was living in a halfway house also trying to get his life together. He was really nice and didn't abuse me in any way. He gave me the most ultimate gift I could ever imagine. We made a baby! Not knowing we did! We became boyfriend and girlfriend in a short amount of time. I kissed him first! And I don't usually do that. We would stay at my apartment a lot, and we'd go to AA meetings together. I was going a lot then.

My brother, Stevie (affectionately called), his wife Anna and I went to a cabin get-away for a few days. I was sitting in the back seat, kinda in the middle talking to Steve and my sister-in-law. She asked me how I'd been feeling, and I told her my breasts were really sore. She gasped, "I bet you're pregnant!" I said, "No, I doubt it." The next thing I know they're looking for a drug store to buy a pregnancy test. Then we stopped at a gas station, me and Anna went to the bathroom. I peed on the stick and in just a few minutes, it pronounced I was indeed pregnant! I was shocked! I was not on any kind of birth control for like ten years. Also, I had heard that some alcoholic women couldn't get pregnant. Because of the drinking. So, I believed that. But low and behold, I wasn't infertile. I just said wow, wow, and wow!! I just thought, "I'm gonna have a miracle baby." Another great miracle from my Lord!

We went on our family trip as planned, and now I was going to be a mom! Praise the Lord, glory be to God. This was going to be a big, big deal in my life now.

I was sober, too. Praise God. But I was smoking cigarettes. I slowed down but didn't really quit, which wasn't good. I moved into a HUD apartment complex by a creek. It was nice. Don, when I told him, was shocked, too, but very excited. We were going to have a baby!

I wanted to know through the ultrasound if I was having a boy or girl. I was going to have a boy – a beautiful boy! And God gave him to me! We were going to be a mom and dad. My mind swirled in many different directions, excited about this new chapter in my life. I lived by myself – did pretty good. My money came from social security disability. And of course, Don helped me too. My best friend Carol gave me a really nice baby shower. I got so much neat stuff. The months flew by, but something not so good was slowly happening. Don got back into drugs (heroin). The worst thing that could have happened at this time in our lives. We got engaged. He had asked me to marry him, and I said yes. That's before I knew about heroin, which drastically changed our future.

The plan was when Hunter was born, I was going to stay at my brother's house and have my mom, Renee, Amy, Carol, and another friend come and help me at different times because I had a C-section.

When my water broke, it was time to go! Steve drove me in his car. I remember laying down in the very back of the SUV and felt every single bump in the road. Ouch! I was miserable back there. I don't remember why I wasn't in the back seat which would have been a lot better. Anyway, I called Don and told him I was going to the hospital. He showed up to videotape. Before he got there, I checked into my room at The Women's Hospital. Very good hospital by the way. I had a private room, and mom, dad, Renee, Amy, Carol, and Steve were all there for me. I was in labor for 12 hours. They tried to give me an epidural, but the curvature of my spine wouldn't allow it. Maybe from my car accident, I don't know. I was going through contractions and had to sit up cross-legged on the table. It was hard and hurt bad. When I was dilating, they couldn't get Hunter out. I was too small; he was too big. So, I had to have a C-section. It messed up all my plans for Hunter being born. I had planned on playing Elton John's song about being a star during the birth. Brought my jam box and cassette, and had it all ready – but no go. It didn't happen like that. I was sad about that, but so overjoyed when Hunter came out healthy.

Meanwhile, his father, Don, got close enough to videotape the procedure. He really wasn't supposed to be in the room. I don't know how that happened, but I have the videotape of my precious son being born.

I looked in a baby name book for my son's name. "Hunter" was the last name of Robert Hunter, a friend of Steve's. I always liked Hunter, so I made it his first name. His middle name is Gabriel, after one of the important Arch Angels in heaven. It's also Hebrew and means "man of God." He's my little miracle Angel baby boy dropped like an unstained jewel from heaven!! This was my baby, and I still say that to this day. I know it was our baby, me and Don's, but he was mine. He was so precious, blonde hair with his dad's blue eyes. Hunter Gabriel was a sweet little angel!

# CHAPTER 26
## STRANGERS

MY FAMILY'S PLAN for me was to stay at Steve and Anna's house because I needed help after the C-section. I got it from my family and friends. My plan was for Don to stay in my apartment, pay rent and live there until I got back, which was about a month. I remember after I had my C-section, I asked the doctor to tie my tubes so I wouldn't have to worry about getting pregnant again (since I was fertile after all). I didn't need another baby being in my 40's. One baby was enough for me, and I knew I would be too old and couldn't give proper care. But I had a miracle baby! It was still hard to believe that I was a mom now. I never thought it could happen.

Don was from Michigan and had a daughter about six or seven at the time. She came in town to meet her little half-brother. My sister Renee had a great album of the time in the hospital, and I had some great pictures, too. I was so big when I was pregnant (my stomach I mean), I couldn't wait to get him delivered. I was breastfeeding him from the start. The best milk for newborns, you know. I remember I got an infection in one of my nipples, and it hurt when he sucked the milk but I endured. Steve and Anna were out of town in France, I believe. They go every summer because Anna's parents and family live there. So they weren't home.

Hunter is part Polish from Donald's side of the family, and my family is German, a little bit of Irish, Indian and European. He was so precious and beautiful. I was starting life as a mother and I was sober! Don came and visited with Hunter at Steve's. When I moved back to my apartment with Hunter on my own, the shit hit the fan. That's when my neighbor told me about Don doing and buying heroin from her husband, who sold it. She would even show me bent spoons in my kitchen from him cooking it up. And when Donald came to see Hunter Gabriel, he would be sitting on my couch nodding off as he was holding him. Don was getting skinny. He was already thin, tall with silvery gray hair. I accidentally saw him naked when he was about to shower, and I was shocked at how much weight he had lost.

So, it happened – I called off the marriage because Don was doing heroin, and I didn't want that around me or Hunter. I might have been a fool with the decision I made because after Hunter was three months, Don went away and NEVER came back! I thought it was because I wouldn't marry him. I'm pretty sure after that Don told his family it wasn't his kid, but he knew Hunter was his.

Anyway, the weirdest part is that not one person in his family except his daughter saw Hunter after that. No phone calls, no visits to see their new little nephew or grandson. Nothing! So that's why I thought that. Don was upset we didn't get married. I could have been wrong all the years that followed, but I couldn't think of any other reason no one ever contacted me, to ask about Hunter or anything.

Then I thought, "Did I make a BIG mistake not marrying Don?" I was an addict, too. Who was I to make that judgment call? Don could have gotten help again. And if we'd gotten married, that would have helped. We would have been a family. I asked myself, "What if?" too many times. How many times did I go back out? Too many. I didn't give him a chance to want to change.

I have cried and cried over this guilt throughout the years, still thinking "what if" or "only if." Did I rob my precious son of having his father in his life? I'm crying while I'm writing this. It still hurts my heart today thinking about it. I had to pray and pray, and still pray to forgive myself and get over the guilt.

# CHAPTER 27
# A NEW BEGINNING

S

O, IT WAS me and Hunter alone in my little HUD apartment. At one point in time, we moved in with Renee and her boyfriend Calvin. They fought all the time, and I worried about Hunter. Then, Renee and I disagreed on how to handle Hunter when he cried when I put him to bed. Renee wanted to pick him up, but I didn't want him to be spoiled and not sleep. So we argued and it reached a breaking point. I got mad and shoved all the stuff on her coffee table onto the floor. She told us to leave. I was kinda glad because Renee and Calvin fought so much, yelling at each other. I put all our stuff in my car along with my precious son, drove to a gas station pay the phone, and called Steve crying about what happened. He said to come to stay with them, so we did (temporarily).

We went to Steve and Anna's. Hunter was only a few months old. They said I had to look for a job, so I started looking in the Greensheet. Back then, they had a lot more job ads. I found a nanny live-in job in The Woodlands, TX. When I talked to Grady, the father, about the job, I thought this is where I needed to go. He was a single dad with one daughter. She was about 10 or 11 years old. They lived in a big five-room, two-story house. My job would be to keep the house clean, cook the meals and watch over his daughter. I can't remember her name, so I'll call her "Missy." My memory is not that good, I told you…

Grady said, "Think about it and let me know." It was such a big house and big responsibility. But I took the job because I needed one, and I couldn't stay and live with Steve forever. So I packed my belongings, and we headed for The Woodlands. Always liked The Woodlands, but never dreamed I'd be living there let alone in a nice big house. I knew it was going to be hard on me and Hunter was under a year old. Missy wanted me to take the job because she fell in love with Hunter. *My God, my God, thank you for taking care and providing for me.*

It was a huge endeavor, but the Lord gave it to me so I was going to try my hardest. In the beginning, it was pretty busy and ok. Missy helped me with Hunter. She was a great help. We took photos of baby Hunter a lot. We got him a baby pool and got some of the cutest photos of my blonde-haired, blue-eyed baby boy. Hunter was slow in his ability to walk, so I had a therapist come once a week to work with him. It worked out well.

Hunter was about to be one-year-old, and I threw him a get-to-gether inviting all my family. I had a big birthday banner hung on the staircase and made him a homemade cake. I got the recipe from a magazine. It was a beach scene. So cute! You know how when your precious baby turns one, you want to throw a big party and your baby doesn't even know what's going on. But you're so excited, you want to make it BIG! It's crazy but that's what parents do. His cake had blue dye water for the ocean and gummy bears in lifesaver candy for inner tubes, striped gum for blankets on the shore, and coconut. It was really a unique, cool cake. I set the whole cake in front of Hunter on his high chair and let him have at it. Took photos. It was a great and neat occasion. Had so much fun and Hunter got a lot of neat toys. Grady gave him a little armchair with a western cloth look. He got a lot of awesome gifts from family, but nothing from Don his father. Not even a word or phone call.

I made $200 a week and had my own room upstairs. After a while, with my money, I hired two maids to come every two weeks to help me clean the house. That helped a lot.

Hunter started going to the YMCA pre-school program, and I think he liked it. When he was there and Missy was in school, I shopped for groceries and kept the house picked up spot cleaning. The two maids helped out with the hard stuff like sweeping, mopping, and vacuuming. It was hard taking care of that big house, but I did it for two years. After a while, Missy started misbehaving and talking back to me. That added to the stress.

Then I made a terrible mistake – Grady let his daughter have a friend spend the night, and they were up really late. I went to tell her they needed to go to bed and turn off the TV. She started arguing with me and I slapped her! What a big mistake! She said her dad said they could watch TV, but I didn't listen…then it was too late. She went and told her dad. He said I needed to move out. I felt terrible but kinda relieved because the house was just too much.

While I was still living there, I had to have carpal tunnel surgery. I asked this girl I knew from AA if she could help me out with Hunter and the house. She agreed, but instead of taking care of Hunter and taking him to the YMCA, she was always cleaning upstairs. It bothered me because Hunter, my baby, was more important, but we all got through it.

Now I had to move out.

So, I got another HUD apartment off Woodlands Parkway. It was just me and my baby boy alone in a big world that sometimes was cruel. *Dear God, please take care of us!*

CHAPTER 28

# THE SERPENT RETURNS

W ELL, GUESS WHAT? I started drinking again. At first, no one knew because I didn't tell anyone. One evening I was drinking and took some pills, even though I knew you shouldn't mix them. We took our Chihuahua "Cricket" for a walk. At one point, I fell down hard and scraped and cut my knees real bad. A couple of girls helped me up; I couldn't get up on my own. They walked us back to our apartment. It was awful and so unfair to my precious Hunter. I don't know how or when it happened. I was probably in a blackout. Steve came over and removed Hunter from the situation. He stayed with Steve and Anna both times when I drank. The last time was January 12, 2007. Hunter was seven. They say every time you go back out, it gets worse, and it really does! I can't forget this incident.

I made tuna fish for Hunter, and he doesn't like tuna fish. I couldn't even feed my son something he liked. And I wasn't cooking. I only wanted to drink, and Hunter had to see his mom in that condition. He remembered, too. A friend told me later that I was lucky that no one saw us when I fell except those two girls. They could have called CPS and reported me. I'm so grateful to God that didn't happen. If Hunter ended up in foster care, that would have been a terrible thing!

I talked to Steve on the phone. He knew I was drunk. Steve drove from Houston to our apartment in The Woodlands. By the time he got there, I was pretty messed up. Steve wanted my car keys (I had driven while drinking with Hunter in the car…so grateful nothing ever happened). I remember I grabbed my keys and ran to my room, threw them up in my closet. I'll never forget what Steve said to me that hurt my heart. He called me a bitch. He found my keys. I was hurting my poor son's heart and putting him in a dangerous situation. The next thing I knew, they were gone. I was in a drunken stupor and didn't care. Actually, by that time, all by myself, I just wanted to drink myself to death. I wanted to kill myself through alcohol poisoning. I didn't have my car keys, but there was a liquor store not far from my apartment. I walked over there and bought a bottle of rum and diet coke and started my suicide trip. So I thought. I even soiled myself and didn't even clean myself up.

The next thing I remember was being helped into an ambulance and laying down. I blacked out again. I woke up in the hospital in restraints. I couldn't move and got very angry. I was cussing, screaming saying, "Get these f---ing restraints off me." The more I screamed and yelled, the longer they kept them on.

What happened was Joe (my ex at the time) came over, I guess to check on me. He saw my door wide open and my dog running around. I didn't even care if someone came in and robbed me or something worse. I would have fought them off. That's how upset and angry I was with myself. I wasn't afraid of anything and very angry and depressed.

Anyway, Joe is the one who called 911. He basically saved my life. My alcohol level was very high, close to alcohol poisoning. Joe did save my life! Otherwise, I might have died, which is what I wanted, but God had something more for me to do. So I'm glad I didn't die that night. Then I remember Joe calling Steve. He told me it was Steve on the phone and put the phone to my ear. I remember saying "Steve" really loud and then yelling "get the restraints off of me." Joe took the phone back, told Steve where I was then hung up. I didn't get to talk to my brother, but I was too busy yelling and screaming about the restraints. It wouldn't have helped anyway – I was out of my mind!

Joe was a con man and conned me out of a lot of my money. He was slick and smooth, kind of a big guy, good-looking but was bald and wore a wig – hehe. He told me lies. I believed him and did some not-so-good things.

He lived with me and Hunter for a while but would bitch about no sex and me not cooking. He bought me a Honda and said he'd make the payments but never did. I was angry with him. I'm so gullible. I believed every lie he told me. But, he saved my life, so I had to forgive, which took a long time. I hated men after all my bad relationships. Forgiveness was hard for me to do at that time in my life. He never did hit me....

CHAPTER 29

# THANK GOD, A BRILLIANT STAR

BACK TO THE hospital – when I awoke the next morning, I finally had the restraints off. Thank God! My younger sister Amy came and saw me. She told me I was going into yet another treatment center…at almost 50 years old. How sad. All my life struggling with alcohol. Yes, I had periods of sobriety, but not much compared to my time drinking. So I was there for a few weeks. Everybody who smoked looked forward to our cigarette breaks, including me.

After that, I went to The Right Step, a 30-day detox and counseling center. I stayed my 30 days. I remember Steve and Anna brought Hunter to see me. It was somewhat nerve-racking at times because Hunter didn't say much, but we played basketball together.

I forgot to mention Gizmo, our dog that Hunter's dad gave to me like a puppy. He was so cute. He was a mix of poodle and Maltese terrier. His whole name was "Gizmo Honeybear Coconut Moondoggie" – he grew up with Hunter. He died at almost 18 years old, at home with us. I had him cremated. His ashes are in a little brown wooden box with his name on it. Today, I also have some of my mom's ashes in a little acorn container and my real dad's ashes. My stepfather was buried in New York, where he's from, by his mother.

After the Right Step, I went to The Next Step (the next stage of treatment). In Spring Branch in another converted apartment complex. This complex didn't' have a pool, and I wasn't about to make any stupid mistakes like the last one I got kicked out of. I was serious about my sobriety this time and had a beautiful son! His hair grew darker and got curly (real curly). Hunter lived with Steve, Anna, and their daughter, Sarah. They brought him to visit me on occasion. He was growing up into a fine young man. Steve got him into Cub Scouts, and he went all the way through, going on a lot of camping trips. Hunter loved them. Steve got him a camping hammock, and he would tie the ends to two trees and sleep in the air off the ground. He loved it! He went to Colorado and Hawaii with the Scouts when he got older. I went a couple of times on camping trips, but I felt too uncomfortable. It was mostly dads, you know. Some moms, but I felt alone because Hunter was off doing Boy Scout things with his friends. I tried socializing but ended up not going anymore. Plus, Hunter was getting older. He didn't want me around. And I'm proud to say, he stayed in it (thanks to Steve). He was very involved, too. He became an Eagle Scout! The top honor for a Boy Scout. I'm so proud of him. The ceremony was great!

Now back to The Next Step – I was taking bi-polar meds and staying sober. Months flew by. Steve helped me pay for some of it, and I paid the rest with my social security disability insurance (SSDI) that I got every month. I got to the point where I could leave and work. I lived there for almost eight months. Then, I found an apartment not far, and by the freeway, all bills were paid. They (Foxhall was the name of complex) had a special where you got so much money off the next three months. It worked for me, but I had to have Steve co-sign my lease, which he did.

My dear twin brother Stevie has done so much for me and paid a lot of money (like for treatment centers). There weren't a lot of free ones. How can I ever repay him?? When I become rich and famous?! Just kidding! The only way I know is to give him love, which I do, and stay sober.

Hunter stayed living with Steve, Anna, and Sarah. Sarah is only one and a half years younger than Hunter. They even looked like brother and sister. So, they grew up together. It was probably better than being the only child. They had each other to play with. They both attended Frostwood Elementary at Gessner and Memorial before it was remodeled and rebuilt.

I would go over to Steve and Anna's house in the evenings to visit with Hunter before he went to bed. I'd lay next to him in bed until he fell asleep. Sometimes I would doze off.

Hunter went through some difficult times. He started acting out with me, wanting to fight or hit me. I can only imagine it was from his hurt I put him through when he was with me and I was drinking. We even went to Colorado (Steve paid to have us fly there) to a parent/child event about children with alcoholic parents. It was intense. But it didn't seem to diminish Hunter's behavior, he still acted out at times. Sometimes, when I took him back to Steve's, he wouldn't get out of the car and just cry. He wanted to stay with me but had to go back to Steve and Anna's.

So Hunter went through a lot of emotions, my precious son. I felt a lot of guilt and it was hard on me, too. Steve even paid for counseling for Hunter, but that didn't seem to help. He was seeing this one man for a while. Hunter was around eight years old. He didn't like this man and ended up getting in a fight with him, hit him, and never wanted to back. It was a difficult time.

# CHAPTER 30
# MY BEST AND LAST HUSBAND (THIRD TIMES A CHARM!)

I WAS ATTENDING AA meetings quite frequently and got a job as a hostess at Pappy's Café. I was their hostess for seven years. Wow, the longest job I ever had! I got a one-bedroom apartment for when Hunter stayed with me, and paid my rent and stuff with my salary and my SSDI.

I was pretty content having my own apartment and being responsible. Hunter would stay with me like every other weekend, and we'd switch up the holidays with Steve and Anna. I had him some throughout the summers. Anna and Steve were pretty strict. Hunter grew up respecting them but not me. Again, thinking of the guilt of what I had done to him. I think Hunter acted out subconsciously not even realizing it. My poor angel boy.

The many relationships and different men in my life affected me because it kinda screwed me and Hunter up. I would get involved with some guy in AA…that hardly ever worked out either. It took a long time to forgive myself even though I knew God had forgiven me. Thank you, Lord!

It was 2010 and Hunter was ten years old. It's easy to remember

– he was born in 2000, so whatever year it is, that's how old Hunter is. I had stopped smoking cigarettes (on and off) and wanted one but didn't have any. So I decided to walk over to the AA club to bum a cigarette. It was just across the street from my apartment complex, Cedar Branch. Do you know how there's a reason for everything that happens in God's world? I was about to have a divine intervention…I met my third(and last husband) and didn't even know it.

I was walking through the parking lot to cross the street to get to the AA meeting, and low and behold – there was this guy hanging out by the washateria/pool area in the parking lot. He had a beer in one hand and a cigarette in the other, so I thought instead of walking all the way to the AA Club, I could just get a cigarette from him. His name was Michael Zellner. He said, "Sure, I'll give you one." He ended up giving me the rest of his pack.

He had just moved in and his apartment was upstairs right across the parking lot from me. When we were on our patios, we could see each other. He was so nice and it was kinda like we had a kindred spirit between us. It was so easy to get to know him. Almost like we knew each other before, like in another life. And we felt comfortable around each other. He was tall, not real tall but taller than me (I was 5 ½'), dark and very handsome.

We became fast friends. I would look forward to him coming home from work (he was a machinist/grinder, which I didn't know what that was). Anyway, I'd meet him in the parking lot between our two apartments.

I really started liking this guy and him, me. So, we started a courtship. Hunter said, "Why don't you get married, mom? I want you to be happy." I thought that was so sweet. So, in 2013, we did! We moved into a three-bedroom apartment in the back family section. Lots of little kids.

I had Gizmo Moondoggie and Michael had a black and white terrier mix named "Marble." Now Marble didn't really get along with other dogs, but he did with Gizmo. Maybe like another kindred spirit between them. It was cool!

# CHAPTER 31
# WEDDING CHIMES

WE WENT TO Chapelwood United Methodist Church. Steve joined the church a while back and kept telling me, when I was still out drinking, about a service called "Mercy Street." It was a different service in the Fellowship Hall, separate from the regular church services in the Sanctuary. It was on Saturday nights at 5:30. I finally started going.

When I met Michael, he was drinking beer. But two days later, he went to an AA meeting with me and quit drinking – hallelujah!! And is still sober to this day. I've been sober since January 12, 2007. I think I was in love.

We got married in the chapel of our church, and our pastor did the ceremony.

Michael has six kids; four of them attended with two grandkids from his daughter, Melissa. Mark and Jessica (his two stepkids) didn't come, but he raised them as his own. Their biological father was in prison. Michael was a good man. He moved furniture for like 15-20 years and did his best raising six kids.

Mark went to school in Washington DC and now is an engineer. Nice guy!

Michael has Spanish, white, and black mixed in his family. When everybody gets together, it's a pretty big crowd. Jessica, his stepdaughter, has four kids. Melissa has Alicia and Anthony – their dad was in prison for a while too, I think. They're 13 and 11 now. And I'm a step-grandmother! Never thought I'd be that either. Hunter now has four stepsisters and two stepbrothers. Wow! From an only child to now having six stepsiblings!

Samantha now has a five-year-old daughter named Amelia Daisy. She calls me "Steffy." So the family is growing even more. I have three step grandkids that I see pretty much. We hardly see Jessica's kids. Only on holidays or birthdays. So, I have more grandkids. I never dreamed my life would turn out like that, but I'm glad!

Katherine is going to be a lawyer. Well, I would say she is one now. She's supposed to graduate in May 2020, but with COVID 19 pandemic, it will be postponed until July.

As the writing of this now, we are going through the Coronavirus pandemic and today's date is March 31, 2020.

It's also the anniversary of my car accident in 1972. Boy, it's been a long time, and I will celebrate the life God has given me and be very grateful for the person I turned out to be. And that I'll be 62 May the 7th and I'm STILL ALIVE. Thank you, Jesus! I trust in you. 2 Corinthians 5:7 – *"We walk by faith, not by sight."*

Our wedding was great. The ceremony was small and some friends from Mercy Street came. Tracy, my dear friend, was my maid of honor. Dawana, my friend and coworker at Pappy's Café, took bunches of photos for us. Fran, her mom, also came. My family came and that was very important to me. We had the date set because that's when our pastor Greg Taylor had time to do it. It was beautiful and just what we needed! Thank you, Jesus!

# CHAPTER 32
# THE CRUISE AND OUR MOM

GUESS WHERE WE went on our honeymoon (funny they call it that)? On a Carnival Cruise! For a week. We had so much fun! Never had been on a cruise and over the course of time, we went on two more cruises. How we did it, I don't know. We weren't rich, you know. Shortly after Michael and I met, I started letting my hair grow back out. It was short. I think on our second cruise I had my hair braided on the side in Jamaica. I loved it! It gave me such a different look and was so much fun. When we came home, I went back to work and thought I was so sassy. I was able to leave the braids in for about two weeks (wash gently). That was a fun time. My initials are S.A.S. with a "Z" on the end now. SASZ was my name! When Michael and I married, Hunter was 13 and was the ring bearer. He wore a white suit with a pink bowtie. He looked so handsome. I wore a backless pale pink chiffon, off-the-shoulder dress that was long in the back and short in the front. I bought it at David's Bridal store. Michael was super handsome in a grey suit with a pale pink tie. And my sweet mother was there. I was so happy she could come.

My mom lived at Brookdale, a senior assisted-living complex, for several years. She had Parkinson's disease – a chronic long-term, degenerative disorder of the central nervous system. In my mom's final stages, she got very weak. Once a week, I would do her shopping. There was a Walmart around the corner.

The end of her life was coming, so hospice became involved. Steve was coming back from France early because we knew mom didn't have much time left. Our siblings came at different times to see mom. Steve got back in time and played some of mom's favorite music – like Johnny Mathis and Tom Jones' "She's A Lady," old favorites.

Our mother passed in the early morning of January 1, 2017. Steve was sleeping there and was with her when she passed on to heaven. My beautiful mother – rest in peace!

# CHAPTER 33
# LAST OF PAPPY'S

I WAS STILL WORKING at Pappy's, but it was pretty shaky. I had somehow torn the meniscus in my left knee. I think from all the running and walking fast at Pappy's. I did the lunch shift, and we stayed very busy. I just wanted to get the customers seated as soon as possible. You don't mess with hungry people. ☺

Anyway, I had the surgery and was off work for about five months. When I went back, things just weren't the same. I was worried about my knee. Could I do the same thing again? No, I couldn't. I started having mental issues and missing work, or couldn't get there on time. And then my precious mother died. I was a mess!

It got to the point that I just didn't go in or even call anymore. They were probably tired of my excuses. Anyway, that was the end of my seven-year career at Pappy's Café. I got to know a lot of regulars working there.

To this day, I still run into customers at the grocery store that remembers me as the hostess at Pappy's Café and smiles! It makes my day! And when I cut my hair short again, they still remembered me. What an honor that is for me. Honor and peace they shall receive.

I fill the Holy Spirit with me right now, I have to write this:

Today (April Fool's Day 2020, as a matter of fact), I went to Bio-Life (where you donate plasma). I was going to start doing it, but I had to pick up paperwork for my doctor to sign. I had to wait, wait and wait. I said to myself, "Why to take so long just to pick up some paperwork?" They said they had to check my vein in my right arm because it was skinny.

She went back to check with the manager, I guess. I waited. She came back and said, "I'm sorry, it's a 'no' at this time. You could check with our other locations." I said, "This one is far out to me enough as it is." I was so frustrated! It was only in an emergency to use my right arm. I had a good vein in my good (left) arm, but a faint one in my right arm so they couldn't use it. I was upset. Why couldn't they make an exception? I cried when I got home. So much for my anniversary yesterday.

Then I finally realized that Jesus was with me and beside me, and there was a reason that door closed. My thinking was He was protecting me from something.

Anyway, I got over it after a good nap. No money-making there.

Since we're going through the Coronavirus pandemic, lots of places are closed. Restaurants – to-go orders only, office buildings and schools closed. No traffic on the freeways. We're not under "lockdown" like some other places, but they advise you to stay home through April. Only grocery stores, pharmacies, and some virtual doctor appointments. It's crazy. This, I will remember! This virus, this plague I think it's the sign of the times. It's here and maybe for a while.

# CHAPTER 34
# HUNTER, MY BELOVED SON

HUNTER LIVING WITH his Uncle Stevie and Aunt Anna, who is from France, got to go with them to France every summer to visit Anna's family in Corsica. He's probably been at least seven times. Hunter is part of their family, too! He has two homes — theirs and mine. He got really good at packing from one home to the other. When he'd come to stay with me, he'd bring his backpack with all his clothes, camera and stuff in it. I had to share him, but it was for the best.

I was a single mom and struggled, and Hunter had a good home there. So he continued to live with them until he went to college. He graduated from Memorial High School and is going to college at Southwestern University. It's a private school in Georgetown, about a half-hour drive from Austin, Texas.

We got him moved in August of 2019. Now, because of the virus, his college is closed down. They all are. He has to move out of his dorm on April 13th. School has closed for the rest of the school year. Wow! Every student is doing online studies, and parents (lots of them) are working from home.

*Please God, help us get this virus under control. Do this kind of things happen for population control? It's really a waste of time to worry; that's an insult to God. God's way surpasses all understanding! We're not to ask why, and so many times I have. God's ways are not our ways, and He works in supernatural, mysterious ways. No one knows for sure what will happen from this pandemic. God's ways are not our ways, and He is in control.*

Hunter is an acclaimed photographer and guitarist. Wow, is he good! He took photography through high school. Uncle Stevie paid for him to take another class before high school. Plus, in the summer when he wasn't in France, he worked for a professional photographer doing the lighting and developing photos. So he knows a lot about that business. He's taken some very nice photos!

And the guitar – my son is an artist at it. He started taking guitar lessons when he was like nine or ten years old. He stayed with me every Tuesday night. I would pick him up from school, take him to his lesson at ABC Music, and wait for him…it was only a 30-minute lesson. I'd just wait for him in my car. The ABC closed down and he went back to rock. He went to many lessons and can play very well. At Southwestern, he is taking classical guitar lessons with maybe jazz later. He even got a classical guitar for Christmas. I didn't know they had a certain guitar for that kind of music. It's a little smaller than a regular acoustic guitar. He has two electric guitars and even a mandolin! He dabbles in all sorts of sounds and has many guitar pedals. He is a talented musician. And I'm so proud of my boy!!

Hunter and Michael got along ok in the beginning, he was thirteen when we married, then the teenager in him came out. He would have fits sometimes and walk away when I was talking to him. I felt disrespected.

It was night and day in his two different homes. Anna and Steve were stricter than I was. I think he held in a lot when at Steve's home and acted out over at ours. It's hard raising a teenager, even in a joint effort. So, we had a lot of talks about it. He would do good for a while then disrespect me again. I told him he was mean to me and it really hurt my feelings. He tried to understand. Now, he'll be twenty years old on June 17th, 2020. My young man has grown a lot and been through a lot, especially when I was drinking. So glad that's over. I've been sober for 13 years now, and that is a miracle. I was in and out, in and out for so long. I was too stubborn to stop. Each time I went back out and drank again, I thought I could control it – this time. But no, I couldn't. I knew I was an alcoholic…but for a long time, I couldn't admit to that.

I do have a concern for Hunter because it runs in the family – the alcohol. My dad, my mom's mom and father, and me. My twin brother drinks, but he's not an alcoholic. And he drinks every day.

I used to think I got all the bad traits – the alcohol and the mental illness, and anger and fighting when I drink.

But I'm ok now. I see a very good doctor and am on good medications. And I just don't drink. I was a drunk and the good Lord saved me! I do smoke as I call it medical marijuana. It's illegal and I don't have a doctor's note, but it's medical for me. It helps with my anxiety and pain. I call it my A.A.T. (attitude adjustment time). I don't believe it's a sin. It grows in the earth and God made the earth. People smoked it way a long time ago, the Indians may be in their peace pipes, and people before that. I don't think it's wrong, but young people should not smoke it. They're growing up and their brains are developing, and you shouldn't mess with that! I'm almost 62. My brain is done.

Well, enough of that!

When Hunter got in his teenage years, he and Michael, my husband, didn't get along very well. They hardly ever talked, and Hunter would just stay in his room. He would only come out to eat or go somewhere. And he ate in his room.

One time, they had a big fight over cleaning his room. Michael got in his face and said "F--K YOU" three times. Hunter stood his ground and didn't try to hit him or push him away or anything. I was so proud of my boy for standing up to him.

Michael was going through some emotional distress and would get depressed. Finally, he went to see his doctor and was prescribed Cymbalta, an anti-depressant. I take it, too, and have been for a long time. It made such a big difference in his life. I wanted him to get on something for a long time, but he didn't want to then. Before, he would get in these moods where he wouldn't say anything to me or

Hunter. He would go all day without saying a word to me, sometimes two days. That drove me crazy, and I would get depressed. So, the situation doesn't happen anymore, and I'm so glad! Now, he calls it his "happy pill" and takes a higher dose than me! But I have Loxapine that I take before bed, and it helps me sleep well, too.

# CHAPTER 35
## THE VIRUS

Now we're just hanging on. Michael lost his job on December 20, 2019, and hasn't worked since. He did get a job that lasted three days but couldn't do it cause the math was too complicated. He said he cried all the way home and also when he got home. That was sad to see him so down.

It's April and he still hasn't found a job. We're both allergic to technology, so doing online applications and sending in your resume is frustrating. The young adults do it like it's second nature to them. I never was good on the computer, and I'm slow – which doesn't help.

Michael's going crazy sitting at home, and it would be worse if he didn't have his meds.

I've been looking for a job for a long time. I put a flyer up in this Adult 50+ apartment complex to be a Personal Shopper or take them to the doctor, or whatever. A friend who lives there suggested it. Michael and I looked there to live, but it has a motel-like hallway and no patios.

We like where we live now – The Lofts at Spring Lake. We have a big private patio with a gate that we can lock. Ours is the very first apartment when you drive through the gates. There is a lake in the back and lots of ducks. When I was younger, we'd go there and mess around.

It was called "The Sand Dunes" back then. That was like in the 1980s. Now, we're living on the property! We have a fireplace and huge living room, two bedrooms and two baths. And I have the master bathroom, which is actually smaller than Michael and Hunter's bath. But it's just right for me!

We moved from where Michael called the "ghettos" off Blalock, upstairs for five years. It was hell walking up and down these steep stairs with both my and Michael's knees. I had to walk down sideways after I hurt my knee. Now we live downstairs. Hallelujah!

We don't know how much longer we can stay in our apartment because the rent is much more. My family and Michael's kids have helped us out a lot. Especially Michael's daughter Katherine (the lawyer-to-be). A business lawyer once she takes the Bar. Anyway, she has paid our rent like three times, and Melissa also helped with her income tax money. I feel like we're in limbo not knowing what will happen. We'll probably have to end up moving. We also had help from our church and other social sources. We have all our bills, including two car payments. Only God knows the future and what will happen. And He has been providing for us. Amen!

We get food stamps, and Michael got a free cell phone! He hasn't had one in like two years. He didn't want one, but now he needs one for jobs and stuff. He has a landline home phone, but we can't pay our cable bill. We're two months behind. When they shut it off, it will be bad (no TV); but because of the Coronavirus pandemic, they have extended the internet so people can communicate with family and friends since they're supposed to stay home. So, that has helped.

I have a feeling this may go on a lot longer than people think. It's really affecting the community. I pray all my extended family will not get the virus.

Hunter got a job delivering food from grocery stores and restaurants. I'm going to try and do that too. The only thing is the delivery to customers. What if it's downtown?! I don't go downtown. I get too lost even with my GPS. I still get confused with that darn thing. I think I'll try to go online for Walmart. Maybe I could do something there? Hunter can help me.

Michael's daughter, Melissa, sent us a YouTube video of how to make a mask for our face out of bandanas. You fold it longways all the way up then put rubber bands, string, or hair ties on each end, then tack one end in the other. Presto! You've got a face mask. My bandana has colorful different emoji's on it. I even got a compliment about mine from an employee at Kroger. Michael had an "I love Jesus" one. They work great! I use rubber bands and it fits perfectly. So, we use them when we go to the grocery store or else when I go buy a BLU refill for my vape.

# CHAPTER 36
# A HOME CALLED HEAVEN

Yes, I vape. Just the small one that you change up. With only 2.4 nicotine, the lowest one I can find. It's like a dang security blanket for me. I only have one that works, and if I misplace it, I have a fit. Another thing I'm addicted to. I do have an addictive personality, and it's hard not to do it. I cough sometimes but not often because it's so low in nicotine. It seems like I have to have something in my hand at all times. I'm so weird –

I start my day early - sometimes I wake up at 4:30 am. Sometimes I go back to bed if I have to take Marble out. But most of the time I stay up.

I make myself a coffee (another thing I'm addicted to) and read my devotionals.

I read the Upper Room that I get from church. I really like the Upper Room. It starts with a title, a scripture, then a story written by different people around the world. I love the stories! There's a thought for the day, a prayer for the day, and a prayer for the day in the end. It comes out every two months.

I also have a small hardbound book called Jesus Calling by Sarah Young. It's like brand new and originally cost $15.99, but I got it for

$2.00 at MAM Resale shop! It's also a devotional for every day of the year. It's so special because each day Jesus is talking to you directly with His thoughts and insights and how to live in this crazy world. And includes scriptures from where the author found them in the Bible.

My faith has led me to realize that spiritual awakening is an ongoing process. I have a picture plaque that says that I got years ago at an AA shop in Spring, TX.

My faith is attached to me more so now than when I was so detached from God through all my drinking days. There were times I was with God in prayer and spirit (lots of prayers), but most of the time I felt displaced because I didn't know where I fit in this great big world. But I realize now that Jesus was with me through it all. And I'm so overjoyed to know that. He was really there all the time. I believed it looking back now at my life, because I could have been dead many times. There is a purpose for every human being on this planet, and the hidden power believed to control what will happen in the future. That's destiny and fate. Our main purpose for everyone is to share the gospel – the teaching or revelation of Christ. The record of Jesus' life and teaching in the first four books of the New Testament – Matthew, Mark, Luke, and John. These chapters speak directly to us readers about what Jesus said about sowing the right seeds and expecting great things to happen. And love others as you would yourself. But that's hard to do when you don't love yourself. I went through many years not loving myself. No wonder I couldn't have a lovable relationship with anyone…and we were usually drinking. How could I have a healthy relationship with anyone like that? I didn't. Through my trials and tribulations, Christ has taught me that there can be a great victory! We have a good God who cares and loves us so very much.

The trials we have to go through are a set-up, not a set-back (as Joel Olsteen would say) of where the Lord wants to take us. Our Destiny!

When we sin, there are always consequences. They may take us away from our decision to follow Christ. But God can redeem us if we let him. He will not force this upon us. God is a respectful God. And He gave us free will, meaning we make the choice! Do we obey or not? Do we sin or not? It is our minds that make that decision. Don't forget about your heart. What is in your heart will eventually come out of your mouth. Sometimes it can take years! But it will. It does.

My heart has happiness and gratefulness for Jesus being by my side all my life, especially in my past dangerous situations. I'm ALIVE! And He loves me, and He loves you.

The King of Heaven wants me and wants you, too. He wants all of us and all of us to obey him. The joy of living in His presence outshines all other pleasures.

It's a much happier life, I promise you. Mark 12:30 says:

*"Love the Lord your God with all your heart,*

*all your soul, all your mind, and all your strength."* †

## CHAPTER 37
# GOD OR LUCIFER?

THERE WILL ALWAYS be trials and tribulations in life whether it comes from God or Lucifer (the fallen Angel). Whatever you go through will build your character and make you stronger. It all depends on if you believe and your attitude! God was by my side all along. Just like my imaginary friend Speedy on his horse, always beside me, even riding beside the school bus.

You have to will your mind not to worry and think positive. That's not easy to do. You have to be calm and trust God. He's the only one that knows the outcome. We may think we do, but anything can happen in this world. Our Lord Father wants no one to go to hell. Besides, hell was made for Lucifer and a third of the angels he took with him after he was thrown out of heaven. Lucifer was a very important and divine angel. But he let pride get in the way and thought he could do a better job than God of running the universe. Can you believe it?!! Well, it's true, and God hates self-pride the most. If you're the kind of person who thinks they know everything, well, you don't and far from it. Parts of the Bible are missing. Can you imagine what else it says that we don't know about?!

God wants us to be free.

John 3:36: *"And anyone who believes in God's Son has eternal life.*

*Anyone who doesn't obey the Son will never experience eternal life but remains under God's angry judgment."*

Hell was meant for Satan, but unbelievers will be thrown in the lake of fire if they don't believe the true story of Jesus. All are judged according to their deeds.

Revelation 20:14.15: *"Then death and the grave were thrown into the lake of fire. This lake of fire is the second death. And anyone whose name was not found recorded in the Book of Life was thrown into the lake of fire."*

So, you see, hell is a real place, and I don't want to spend my eternal life there. I'm not afraid to die. I just don't want to have to suffer. I don't think anybody does, but in this crazy world, people are already suffering living day-to-day. We have all suffered in our lives at one time or another. But I don't want to suffer in the lake of fire for sure. That's forever! I'd rather be with Jesus in heaven!

Psalm 91:9-10: *"If you make the Lord your refuge, if you make the Most High your shelter, no evil will conquer you; no plague will come near your home."*

The Coronavirus will not touch - I pray - my extended family, relatives, and friends. We will be like invisible. So many people are dying.

I wonder if this is a way to control the population in the world when it gets too overcrowded?? I don't know. Only God knows. Just like only God knows when Jesus is coming again. From heaven through the clouds on a white stallion! It will be so glorious! I do think when He comes again (Jesus) it is closer than some might think, for those who believe. Probably not in my lifetime, but maybe my precious son's life. Anything can happen –

# CHAPTER 38

# ONLY GOD KNOWS, MY RESCUER

---

## Another Story
## My experiences at New Life in Christ in Willis, Texas

I DON'T FOR SURE remember (maybe my brother does), but I think I admitted myself at New Life in Christ in Willis, Texas. I was basically homeless. I had just broken up with this guy. I'll just call him a guy. I don't remember his name and don't want to. He was a construction worker and in most jobs, he'd be topless. He had a nice chest and was tan and looked ok. I remember he would bleach his hair blonde and was very hyper. We met, drank, and were together for a while. His mom lived in a mobile home, and we'd go over there and drink.

The next thing I knew, we moved into a small one-bedroom mobile trailer. Very small. So we drank, had sex, and fought a lot. One evening I was trying to light our small gas oven to cook. I was drunk and got too close to where you light it. It blew. I moved back but singed some of my eyelashes off. They were really short for a long time until they finally grew back. I brought some of my clothes and things. But the most valuable things I had with me were my photo albums. My photos of South Padre Island (a long time ago) and a baby album my mom made of me.

There's a reason I'm telling you this. We broke up. There was some time before I could get back to the trailer to get the rest of my things after I started going to New Life in Christ. My mom drove me there. It was embarrassing for my mom to see where I was living, but I couldn't change it.

Anyway, the first place I went to was the outside shed behind the trailer and looked for my photo albums. Ahh – I found them and opened one up. The photos were gone! I opened the next one – the same thing – all the photos were gone. I had a stack of photo albums and in everyone, the photos were all carefully taken out. I was honestly shocked. I couldn't believe it. That guy took the time to take out the photos but leave the albums. It was a cruel joke. I knew my mom was upset, too.

You never know what life brings your way. And it's not always pleasant.

So I enrolled in this program, New Life in Christ. I really wanted to change my life and love Jesus with all my heart.

I thought this would be great for me. We lived in dorms, like little houses with bunk beds. There were me and two other girls. That's all! But it was a small organization and the owners, a couple, (whose names I'll keep anonymous) lived in a nice, big one-story house. Lots of land around.

There was another church-type organization not far from us led by this oriental man, who I had a big crush on. We went to some of his services, and they were really good!

Anyway, back to the home (my new home for now). It was going great in the beginning. We had Bible lessons, learned scriptures, and did other things like that. We also cooked, cleaned, and kept the outside (yard, shrubs, flower beds) trimmed and cut. Then we had to dust and clean everything in the couple's house. They had a lot of what-nots, china, etc. Pretty but a lot to dust and clean. We spent a lot of time outdoors cleaning, pulling weeds, trimming around the flowers, and mowing. Actually, to tell you the truth, my good arm and hand were getting overworked and started to hurt.

So, guess who they picked to mow their back yard, which was an acre of land? Me! I couldn't believe it. Two healthy girls living there also, and they told me I had to do it. I told them my arm and hand were really sore, so they got me a wrist brace.

Each moment you can choose to practice Jesus' presence or to practice the presence of problems. I want the presence of Jesus in my life, but it was getting really weird around their home.

So, there I was, mowing an acre of their backyard in tears most of the time. Their philosophy was "hard work is good for you." But not when you're in pain…they made me do it anyway. Through my tears, God gave me a poem in my head, and I give him all the Glory. It's called "Letting Go":

*"Dear Father God, please help me to let go, and receive your grace and mercy deep within my soul. That I may know the freedom that will surely set me free; to live my life for you alone and know peace and serenity. For in Your wisdom, You know what's right for me and my life ahead. Please help me learn to give it to You and choose your love and will instead. Please help me learn to loosen the chains that prevent my growth in your love. Please help me learn to give it to You and soar to your heights like a dove. For in your wisdom, You know what's right for me and my life ahead. Please help me learn to give it to You and choose your love and will instead."*

Jesus is Lord and I magnify His name. Glory be to God!

The pain got so bad, I would cry at night in my bed. They finally got me to a doctor who gave me pain pills, but they didn't really give me any breaks. Electricity would shoot down my arm and hurt badly. Their attitude was like, "just take your pills and you'll be fine." But I wasn't fine!

One time, I left the lawnmower out and it rained. The couple's husband came to my dorm and chewed me out bad for leaving it in the rain. I thought, "This man is supposed to be a Christian man, and he sure isn't acting like it." Not even an "I'm sorry" did I get from him.

It was just us three girls for a long time. Wendy, one of the girls, was in love with the pastor's son at the church we went to in Conroe every Sunday and Wednesday. You could tell that girl was smitten with the pastor's son. We set in the front row so she could see him the whole time up pretty close. I think the feeling was mutual, but not sure, so she really looked forward to going to church.

I had been there a few months now, and Wendy was at the point she could work and had a little more freedom. She cleaned homes and apartments and had her own little business. I got to where I could go help her. I just wanted to leave that place. You had a certain amount of time to shower, and if you had to shave, that was bad because you had like ten minutes to shower. If you went over, you got written up. They were strict! Who cares how long you take a shower? I wanted to be clean. It was just ridiculous!

Anyway, one day I went with Wendy to clean houses. When we got back to New Life, she said she was going to drive up the road to empty the trash, which she did daily. But this time she didn't come back…ever! Maybe a month later we saw her in the church we go to. She was sitting by the pastor's son in the front pew. So Wendy left for love. I don't blame her. Now it was just me and the other girl I'll call "Christy." Now Christy was not on my side as far as not liking the place anymore. It was all so weird! She was like a robot at the couple's beck and call. I was in my own room now, and they would still time me on my showers. It was crazy. No wonder Wendy left. I hope she fell in love and they got happily married. I never found out what happened.

Christy was on the couple's side, and it certainly showed. She even started to act like them, like she was a clone.

I painted a gazebo practically all by myself. We were in the middle of building a 24-room dormitory to expand the place. I had to go out to the dorm site every day to sand, paint or do something.

Well, I had had enough. I finally told them I wanted to leave. They didn't like that. I felt all alone with no one to help me.

I wanted to call my brother to arrange for him or someone to come to get me, but they wouldn't let me call anyone! I felt like a prisoner. So they ended up taking me with my suitcase and stuff and just dropped me off at a Conroe outlet mall. No money, no bus ticket, no goodbye. I just cried and cried, but was so glad I was away from that place. It says in the Bible, "leave vengeance to the Lord." Well, a few months later, a tornado hit their area. It destroyed the 24-room dormitory and didn't touch one ounce of the other church organization not far from them that I mentioned earlier. Leave vengeance to the Lord and He will take care of you. They treated me unfairly and God took care of it.

Back at the outlet mall, I thought, "I'll just see if I can find me a job and stay with my mom and dad," who still lived in Conroe. I called my dad and told him what happened. He came and got me, but I didn't stay with them. My dad was drinking, and he told me he was going to drive me to Oklahoma to stay with my half-sister Cathy. My dad had also remarried and had two kids, Cathy and Rick. So, I have a half-brother and sister in Moore, Oklahoma. I didn't want to go. I had like a suitcase and a few things. That's all I had. What happened to all my things? Where were they and where was my home?

That evening, we stayed the night in a motel. The next morning my dad drove me all the way to Oklahoma. And drank most of the way. I didn't want to go, but my dad wouldn't take me anywhere else. I felt stuck again. It was a long and uncomfortable ride. Eight hours! You can't say no to my dad when he's drinking…

# CHAPTER 39
# NO JUDGMENT!

WE GOT TO Cathy's house (my half-sister). I stayed with her for a few months. We got along ok, she just thought she knew about everything. She had some issues about respecting my space. Instead of knocking on the bedroom door, she would just barge right in. I thought that was rude. I got a job as a manager of a tanning salon. With my experience, I'm surprised I got this job. The much younger girls who worked under me would just kinda blow me off. I remember there was this one guy that would come and tan, his's face beat red. I told him he shouldn't use the tanning beds so much. Well, he didn't like hearing that and probably complained to my boss because I was fired.

So then I got a job working for a wholesale meat company. They taught me how to learn the computer for the job, and I did pretty well. I was their receptionist, took orders, and printed out orders. It was winter and I froze my butt off. I remember I was driving to work one morning and it was very cold, windy, and sleeting. The roads were slick. I almost had a wreck. My car was sliding on the slick and frozen road, and I had no chains on my tires. Thank God I didn't slide into another car. I hated the cold, and the wind was very cold which made it colder. I wanted to go back home to Houston, but I didn't have a home to go to, so I endured.

I finally got my own apartment and I was so glad. Living with Cathy was a challenge.

Anyway, I met my neighbor Debbie. She was hit by a semi-truck in her car, and her right arm was amputated at the elbow. I thought I had problems – at least I had my arm, so I was grateful. Debbie could do anything. One Thanksgiving, she cooked a whole turkey dinner for her and her sons. She did it all by herself! I didn't think I could do it. We became friends. She is a dear, sweet woman. I wonder what happened to her. I pray for her that she's ok.

I eventually got back to Houston and was so glad. I could not take the weather in Oklahoma. I'm more of a beach person. Love the sunshine! Sunshine from heaven and Jesus, which reminds me of this scripture – John 3:16-17: *"For God loved the world so much that he gave his one and only son so that everyone who believes in him will not perish but have eternal life."* God sent his Son into the world, <u>not to judge the world</u>, but to save the world through Him.

Jesus did not come to judge. Why do so many people believe that? He came to save us, not condemn us. All we have to do is make that choice to believe in Jesus' crucifixion, His burial, and the resurrection, and you will not go to hell. Have eternal life from Jesus and you will live forever with Him in the 1,000 years of peace in this new home and beyond!!

# CHAPTER 40
## THE EASTER EPIDEMIC

TODAY IS EASTER 4/12/2020 with no church to go to worship. The Coronavirus is trying to bring us down, but it won't. God is good! He will get us through this. But it feels empty without being in a church to worship the resurrection of Jesus. It's 6:15 am. I went and sat on our patio and raised my hands (both) for Jesus being brought back from the dead, back up to Heaven to sit on the right-hand side of God, our Creator! To thank Him for conquering death and giving His people new hope and life.

To be born again and follow Jesus. Such a wonderful thought!

*"I want to go back to Jesus loves me this I know, for the Bible tells me, for the Bible tells me so."* From the song *"I wanna go back"* by David Dunn.

Jesus said in John 15:5: *"I'm the vine; you are the branches. Those who remain in me, and I in them, will produce much fruit. For apart from me, you can do nothing."*

So, if I read this and believe in what it says, then I really can do all things through Christ who strengthens me. Without Jesus, I would just be an empty shell wandering around like an idiot.

# CHAPTER 41
# A GENTLEMAN

B**ACK TO BEING** married to the most wonderful man in my life. One thing among others is that Michael has not a jealous bone in his body. It's so refreshing to be with a man who doesn't get jealous or angry when I hug another man, which I do many times (both men and women) at Mercy Street. And he is so respectful to me. He would get so mad at Hunter for disrespecting me. A lot of times. For that matter, anyone who disrespects me. And what a gentlemen Michael is! And so loving. He always opens the car door for me and closes it. We noticed one evening after church (we take a poll) how many husbands or boyfriends opened the door for their women, and only one guy did! Where has chivalry, courteous behavior and just being a gentleman gone?!

It's few and far between these days. And good men are hard to find but not impossible! Girls, get to know their heart, that's a good start!

## A PRAYER

*Heavenly Father, please help me with my hurt. I pray you will forgive me for my addictions to coffee, pot, my BLU e-cigarettes, and shopping. I admit I'm addicted to these and more (thoughts in my mind that are bad).*

*I would probably have a lot less frustrations in my life. I lose self-control or don't care. And it bothers me. A Jesus follower wouldn't act like that, like me, would they? Is that what sin is all about? Because we don't think we can do all the right things? I can't without your help Lord, God my Father. Please help me. My husband Michael wants to know if the mentally ill can hear from God. If you commit suicide but ask forgiveness before you kill yourself, will you go to heaven or hell? So many questions, Lord. How do I deal with it all (please help me understand)? Please deliver me from evil. In Jesus name, amen.*

Today, and have been for a few months, I'm watching TBN on TV. I love to hear the different pastors talk about life, the gospel, and Jesus. Some of my favorite pastors to listen to are (some you may know) Joel Olsteen, John and his son Matt Hagee, Joseph Prince, Joyce Meyer, Steven Furtick, Dr. David Jeremiah, Dr. Charles Stanley, Max Lucado, Robert Morris, Dr. Ed Young and others. I listen more than I watch if I'm doing something, like in the bathroom. And I love it when they all quote scripture. It helps me learn and I do want to learn all about God, Jesus, and heaven. Remember, a spiritual awakening is an ongoing process and that's so true for all eternally. Watching TBN, I learn so much about the Bible and other stories that I hear are so similar to today's events and things that go on in the world. How men and women are still the same in their good and bad deeds as back then – 2, 000 years ago! How amazing!

Just as I can look at His scars and remember either the pain and sorrow or the faithfulness and unchanging love of God who has the power to redeem and renew, transform and restore. Jesus understands our suffering.

# CHAPTER 42
# JUST WHAT IS AN ADDICTION?

IN MY PAST drinking days, I wasn't walking with God, but He was always by my side, holding me as I cried. Soothing me of my torment. I had God on the back burner and ignored Him when I drank. But somehow through it all, I found myself praying for God's help. And He did help me when I was oblivious to it. But he was by my side all along. And for that, I am truly grateful. To me, I was nothing but a drunk. But to God, I was and am special.

When I drank, I didn't take my medications for my bipolar mental disorder. Which, of course, wasn't a very smart thing to do. Alcohol is a depressant so that just brought me down more. I felt my family was disgusted with me so I hardly called when I drank.

This is a reflection of my journal, which is also throughout of my book.

*"I don't want to abuse Your grace, God, I need it every day."* From the song *"Holy Water"* by We the Kingdom

Michael quit smoking cigarettes! Hopefully forever! He's wearing the patch, and I'm sure that helps. He's going to MHMR now to get his meds free and the patches, too. Still unemployed (we both are). But in a way, I think having to stay home kept him away from other people (smokers) where he's not tempted to smoke. That kinda helped.

And I quit vaping the BLU e-cigarette! We are overcomers ("no man can climb out beyond the limitations of his own character," John Morley). Now I smoke straws! Well, not really smoke them, I chew on them to help me get through this patch. Don't knock it till you've tried it! That habit drove me crazy, smoking those BLU's. I would always misplace them, and that drove me crazy…and sometimes I'd get a dud that wouldn't work. That frustrating habit drove me crazy. But the addiction drove me to keep doing it. What do you think about the unhealthy habit that drives one crazy, but you still enjoy indulging in it? That's weird!

I'd think you were a crazy person, but I do it myself and other people do, too.

"Many of us are more capable than some of us, but none of us is as capable as all of us," Tom Wilson. We can do it! Unity!

But I am so very proud of Michael. He smoked for years and years, and just quit with the patch. It was getting so expensive. Just think of the money we'll save now.

What is an addiction? Dr. Jim Jackson defines it as any area of our lives which is out of control – where we are compulsively driven. That sounds familiar, doesn't it?! Also, from one of Jim Jackson's books – "How can our addiction be healed?" The only path I know about is spiritual. Basically, an addiction is anything we use to fill the empty place within our hearts. "This is a void that only one Creator can fill," Jim Jackson. So true, so true – Jim Jackson is my true friend. He was the senior pastor at Chapelwood United Methodist church when I joined Mercy Street. He was not the pastor of Mercy Street but sometimes spoke there. I met Dr. Jim Jackson through my brother, and I just love him. He is the kindest man I know. We had counseling with him at one time about Hunter. I wanted him to come live with me again, but Steve and Anna didn't want that to happen. It was mainly Michael's idea to get Hunter back. I wasn't so sure it was a good idea because Hunter and Michael never had a special relationship, and still don't. That makes me sad. My brother Steve even wrote me a long letter (I still have it) about if I take Hunter back, he couldn't help financially anymore. I guess because he'd be living with me. Long story short, and a lot of counseling, I decided Hunter was better off with Steve and Anna, and he wanted to stay with them. I wanted the best for Hunter, and they could give him more than me.

But Dr. Jim Jackson is a wonderful Godly person to be around, and very good at all he did at the church. And a great counselor! He helped us a lot, then the church sent us to San Antonio – me, Michael, and Hunter – to get away and have fun. We went to the Alamo, Ripley's Believe It or Not, and down the River Way. It was only for a few days but a nice getaway.

He will always be a special and favorite person in my life. He has written books, too, and I have a couple of them. I'm reading More Spiritual Lessons from Life (a Daily Devotional).

# CHAPTER 43
# FROM THE INSIDE OUT

FORGIVENESS MEANS THE action or process of forgiving or being forgiven. Wow! What a mind-blowing definition. How simple an act but can be very hard to do. But what does that actually mean, to forgive? Do you forget too? Are you supposed to? Aren't we supposed to forgive as God has forgiven us? But God forgets and it's gone forever. He doesn't bring it back up or throw it in our faces. It's gone, forever. Can I do that, can we do that and be sincere at the same time? I call myself a believer. Can I truly do that? I know how I can – with the blood of Jesus! But sometimes I have negative thoughts of a person again and an incident comes to my mind, and I want to remind them. But we're not supposed to do that.

You hear about some guy that killed a child because they had too much to drink and had a head-on car crash. The son or daughter is killed, but the drunk guy lives. But the parents choose to forgive him. We have free will and choose what to do with it. "From the inside out, Lord my soul cries out" – Hillsong.

The Lord wants us to be in the image of Him. We have to do it.

If Hunter got killed in a car crash, I don't honestly know if I could forgive the person, or it would take a long time if could I even then get over it. How could anyone get over something like that? But it happens daily – deaths – deaths of loved ones and forgotten ones.

And what about the ones who commit suicide? Are they forgiven? Do they go to heaven? No one knows but our God almighty. Especially the young kids who can't take the bullying anymore, who don't have any friends, who are abused – mentally, physically, or sexually. When they can't take it anymore. Does God understand? Do they go to heaven?

I believe babies go to heaven. They are innocent. We are born a sinful nature. But babies that are aborted don't know anything, and toddlers who are abused or shot in a drive-by shooting aren't old enough to know anything. I think they all go to heaven. Our God is a loving God. And does he ever love us – yes!! Unconditionally!

Have I forgiven my first husband and the others for the abuse I suffered or the rapes that happened to me? Yes, I have. I don't think humans can forget, though. The young ones were just drunk and horny. Mickey G. just had a mean streak in him and didn't respect women of any kind. The other ones did bad things. I was with the wrong men at the wrong time in my life. Was it meant to be? I'm not sure because all sins lead to consequences, so I know when I was drinking, it could lead to bad consequences and usually did. I caused it upon myself because I was not in line with God. The bad things that happened to me were because I put myself in bad situations, not always knowing it. It just happened. Life happens! And you never know what it could be. An earthquake in your city, a big sinkhole appears at a busy intersection, a friend has a heart attack, you get a messy divorce, you're so depressed you want to end your life.

That's why there's Jesus, wonderful Jesus! He died to save you from hell and sin, so you may have eternal life. You only need to believe and accept. You only NEED TO BELIEVE!!!!! It's pretty easy to become a Christian and accept Him in your life, but it can be hard to lead a Christian life. Lots of turns in the road. We need direction, right? To follow Jesus and follow the light. Like a beautiful lighthouse beaming brightly. Whether near or far, it's always there for us to see. Don't leave the rays of the lighthouse and step back into darkness. That's rough living if you ask me. Stay in the light and be bright (and brave). I love lighthouses. But since you can't see a lighthouse in the middle of the ocean, look to the brightest star at night and the sun's gleam in the day and you'll never run out of light. Keep it always on your horizon!

Now I can forgive the men who hurt me in my life. Joe was a con man and jerk, but he saved my life when he called 911. Would I have drunk myself to death that night? Maybe a different intervention would have happened? All I know is that God saved me that lonely night, and I am forever grateful!

I googled "suicide," and these are the scriptures that come up but no mention of the word itself. Read if you like: Exodus 20:13, Acts 24:15, Romans 5:2-5, and 2 Corinthians 1:10. It might be somewhere in the Bible…I just don't know where.

# CHAPTER 44
# SELFISHNESS AND GOSSIP

I KNOW I CAN be selfish, and I'm working on it. I think most people have some of that in them. Good grief, when you're really little, you have to be taught to share. I don't think we're born givers – it's usually "me, me and me" or "me, myself and I" will not share my toys and stuff. But when you do, you usually feel better, the other person feels better…one of the two or both. That would be the best. Scriptures on the subject:

Philippians 2:3 – *"Do nothing out of selfish ambition or vain conceit. Rather, in humility value others above yourselves."*

James 3:16 – *"For when you have envy and selfish ambition, there you find disorder and every evil practice."*

Proverbs 11:25 – *"A generous person will prosper; whoever refreshens others will be refreshed."*

Michael pointed out to be a selfish thing I did the other day. We were watching some dumb videos, so I said I'm turning it to something else. I turned the channel and went in the other room. He said, "Did you see what you just did? You turned off the channel without even asking if I wanted it turned. And got up and walked into the bedroom."

That was selfish. I had no consideration of Michael's feelings. And he says I do it a lot. I don't even think or am aware that I do it. That's bad! I need to be more considerate of Michael's feelings. Why do we do things that we're not even aware that we're doing that could hurt others' feelings? I don't know or realize I'm doing it. I certainly need to check my intentions and think first about what I'm about to do. Don't be think less! Is there such a word? I hope so because it fits!

Anyway, so I deal with selfishness in my own life. We are to refresh each other, not act negatively or talk bad or back to each other. Of course, that can depend on the situation, but the majority of people I think wouldn't want to be talked about. That's gossip and can be very hurtful.

Everybody talks about everybody else. We do it and don't even realize it. A "gossip" means a person who likes talking about other people's private lives. Well, that can come out true or false and can be hurtful or cause negative emotions to erupt. If it's true and positive, well that's good. But gossip can be dangerous. Watch what we say to one another; about one another.

*"God only knows what you've been through; God only knows what to say about you." God Only Knows"* by King & Country.

# CHAPTER 45
## BITTERSWEET

THE OTHER DAY, May 7th of 2020, was my and my twin brother Steve's birthday. We're 62 years old! I'm not going to think of myself as getting old. I mean I am growing older, but I can be young at heart. It's hard to do at times when aches and pains invade. I got a homemade card from my girlfriend Frannie, she's from Mercy Street. The church is closed down until the end of May because of COVID-19, as it is now called.

Frannie took the time and effort to make me this unique card using paper props. She took the time and made it for ME! Wow, that's cool! I felt special. And we can all experience that feeling if we let Jesus in our hearts and lives. What a wonderful feeling. Well, I'm talking about myself, too! Not just you, but we can experience it together. It's better than being alone. Now you can accept Jesus in your heart when you're by yourself, as I've done watching it on TV. TBN is a great one and CBN's 700 Club is a great program. And I listen to them both. A lot of good preaching.

Steve and I didn't get to see each other on our birthday because they were all at the "I'll Fix It" Ranch in Sealy, TX. Their place looks great. Now they have a guesthouse for people to come to visit or stay by themselves. Steve's added on a lot…like a pool with a statue of a big cement pig planter by it. It's awesome!

Anyway, Michael and I were at our apartment, so no get-together. That virus has some people going loco! I wear my face mask when I go to the store. I think everybody is supposed to, but not everybody does. So it was kind of a bummer birthday. But I got well-wishes and my family texted or called me.

Today is Mother's Day 2020. Hunter drove back here from the ranch to stay here for a while. I'm glad he came on Mother's Day — that's special! And, he's paying for us to have pizza tonight. Alright!

Michael is working at UberEats. He's really hustling and making money, but today he got a speeding ticket and then hit a curb while looking at his phone to get directions. What a bummer. $600.00 of his $1,000 check went to fix his car. Thank God we had the money or else Michael would have to use my car…and I need my car.

Give thanks in all circumstances!

I try to look at life like that. Whether good or bad happens, I try to do that. In Michael's circumstance, we are thankful we had the money to fix the car. It depends on which side your mind is on. If it's negative, then we rant and rave about the added expense (which we did do a little of that). Michael's sick about it, but we had to change the channel and look at it in a positive light even after he had to buy two tires. That $1,000 is gone now, but we had the money to fix the car. That's the main thing. Give thanks in all circumstances!

# CHAPTER 46
# THE I'LL FIX IT RANCH

I AM AT STEVE and Anna's ranch in Sealy. Nice little farm/ranch on 40 acres. I just like to call it "The Ranch." It sounds cooler. They've had it for quite a few years now. It started out with a double-wide mobile home, but they have added on and updated a lot! it's a three-bedroom home now. I just love the way Anna decorates. Out here, it's country stuff everywhere. It's very nostalgic!

They have cows, five donkeys (a white one I named "Casper"), goats, two lambs, chickens…and I heard a rooster outside this morning crowing away. I'm writing this at The Ranch, listening to the birds and nature. It's beautiful out here! Last night before dark, Steve and Anna took a walk. I walked some, then I got in the golf cart with Hunter and he drove us around. It was silly and fun. He drove around in circles, driving crazy, and I almost fell off several times. But I was holding on tight, laughing all the way! We were under severe thunderstorm warnings this weekend, but it didn't rain on our parade till the middle of the night. I'm so blessed to have a brother that has a getaway from the city. They also bought a two-story house close to the gravel road, just a short ride from the guesthouse where Hunter and I were staying. They remodeled the two-story house and it looks cool, too. It has a bedroom downstairs and two upstairs. One bedroom has two beds, the other has two sets of bunk beds. Very large room with three bathrooms. Very homey and neat.

They use the guesthouse now for everyone who wants to get out of the city for a few. My brother is on the boards of United Way, Boys & Girls Club, and some others. He books the guesthouse for free to anyone who wants to come!

That's my brother, KIND!

My niece Sarah, Anna, and Steve have been out here for eight weeks because of the COVID-19 pandemic. Out in the country is the best place to stay during this time. If you're able. Steve goes back and forth to Houston for work. Some businesses have opened up, but some still haven't. There have been protests in other states to go back to work. A lot of people have no income. I'm just glad Michael is working!

Anyway, back to The Ranch. Sarah, my beautiful niece, has six new kittens to care for. They have four cats. Two white ones had three white kittens. The other two orange and gray tabbies had two gray and one dark tabby kittens. Their bellies are so full of milk, they roll around. They're so tiny (about 3-4 weeks old). Then there's Scout (their Labradoodle), two black and white dogs – one is a foster and the other dog is The Ranch dog. Don't know who owns him, but he stays with the other dogs. I guess he adopted The Ranch's main house. Hunter and I are staying the weekend and leaving Sunday.

# CHAPTER 47
# A Funky Place

Now I'll admit I can be lazy. I don't like cleaning the house, especially dusting, sweeping, and mopping. I'll vacuum the bedroom carpet. We have wood tile floors everywhere else. Sweeping and mopping hurt my lower back, and I have to take everything off the surface to dust. As I said, I'm lazy. I don't like that I'm like that. The kitchen and my bathroom stay the cleanest, except for the floors. I'm just not a good housekeeper. I think some other people aren't either. I wish I had a maid and our own personal chef. That would be great! Michael and I do cook, taking turns cooking meals. But we're really not that great – does anybody else feel that way??

Enough about being lazy. We have to deal with it in our own way – with the Lord. I keep myself clean. Why can't I keep our apartment cleaner?! I gotta change the channel.

I'm watching Mercy Street on Facebook this Saturday evening (5-23-20). I sure hope they open back up in June. Michael and I really miss going there. I'm so glad we can watch it online. No audience, but Melissa (our pastor), Richard, Sam, the Mercy Street Band, and a few others make this happen. What a blessing!

*"It may look like I'm surrounded, but I'm surrounded by you"* sung by Michael W. Smith. What's it like to be surrounded by God's love?

Michael says he loves Jesus but hates life. What is that supposed to mean? I have bad days, but I don't hate life. Now there were times in my life when I did. I tried to commit suicide. I didn't know Jesus like I know and understand him more now. So many people take it wrong. If you're a believer in Christ, that doesn't mean you're religious. A band, DC Talk, has a song called "Jesus Freak." Well, I want to be a Jesus freak. I have to remember other people may not like it. My purpose in life is to help make Jesus known to everyone I meet. But I don't do that – not with everyone I meet. I like to enter Jesus' name in my conversation with others, which sometimes I do. But other times I don't. I'm not going to be a beggar, I'm not gonna be a pauper because God has many more blessings coming my way. I know that because God loves me and wants the best for me. Your attitude while going through your struggles (as with mine) is like 99% of how you react to the situation. How you perform and act, including me, is not always easy. Like Michael saying he hates life. Is that always true, really?? How can one love Jesus but hate life? He was abused mentally and physically as a child. He had a rough upbringing, out on his own at a young age. He went without food at times. Never could get a good break. Never got ahead. Are there people out there who feel like that? I bet there are a lot out there. I struggled throughout my life. I was abused by boyfriends. I didn't get the best jobs because I didn't go to college.

Some things we bring upon ourselves, out of stupidity, out of lack of knowledge and wisdom. Sometimes because we can't control people, places, and things – the Serenity Prayer: *"God, grant me the serenity to accept the things I cannot change, the courage to change the things I can, and the wisdom to know the difference."*

Boy, do we ever need more wisdom in this world.

# CHAPTER 48
# HELL

ET'S TALK ABOUT hell – some people believe in it and some people
don't. I believe there is a hell. But that place wasn't made for us
as so many might believe. It was made for Lucifer and one-third
of the Angels that rebelled against God and tried to overthrow him.
God wasn't having that and kicked them out as quick as lightning.
They dwell underground where fire and the Lake of Fire are. Satan is
the Prince of Darkness. No one needs to go his way If you don't want
evil. If you believe in the Bible, how could you not believe in hell? The
Bible reads about the defeat of Satan in Revelation chapter 20:7, verse
10: "Then the devil, who had deceived them, was thrown into the fiery
lake of burning sulfur; joining the beast and the false prophet. There,
they will be tormented day and night, forever and ever." And 20:15
says: "And anyone whose name was NOT found recorded in the Book
of Life was thrown in the Lake of Fire." So why would a loving God
throw his people in the Lake of Fire? He doesn't. You make the choice.

If you don't believe in God or want to do things on your own
instead of believing in Jesus and that He rose from the dead after the
third day, SO BE IT! You and I have the choice of free will. Bye, bye,
I'm following Jesus. I want my spirit and soul to live in heaven. Come
with me and go down the chosen path. NOT in the Lake of Fire. In

Jesus' presence, you can face uncertainty with perfect peace. "Believe with me that even the most difficult and painful experiences of our lives can be used for good," as quoted by Dr. Jim Jackson. What the devil means for evil, God can turn into something good. Only God can do that! So, choose your path and if you choose Jesus, hallelujah! Be prepared and be ready. For no one knows the second coming of our beloved Jesus. Only God the Father. And He will set all things straight. Just believe, just believe! After the second coming, there will be a thousand years of peace, no suffering, no murders. Who wouldn't want that? Hell is a real place. He made it for Lucifer and his demon angels. I don't want to go there because it's forever!

In the Bible, it says he prowls around like a hungry lion waiting for someone to devour. Satan, he comes to kill, steal and destroy only! Don't be fooled, demonic spirits are everywhere. You leave a sliver of a window open, and he'll come in your heart uninvited. We have to keep Jesus by our side at all times to keep the devil at bay. The world is under the bondage of sin and evil. Draw closer to Jesus and in His presence, we can face uncertainty with perfect peace.

# CHAPTER 49
# MOTIVATION

H OW ABOUT CHANGING the subject? Whew! The last chapter was deep. And dark. But at the same time glorious because we do have a choice.

I have this calendar that's about motivational quotes that I got from my dear friend and hairstylist, Margarita. I found her shop at Long Point and Hollister called "2,000 Cuts." I was at the Next Step (the extended-stay program) when at a point in time I could go out on my own and work. I found 2,000 Cuts, and Margarita has been cutting my hair ever since. Every year she gets different calendars for her customers, and I like the motivation ones the best. So, I would like to share a few with you. They're really good! Sorry, I can't show the neat photos...

**COURAGE:** "Everything you've ever wanted is on the other side of fear." – George Addair

**SOAR:** "Kites rise highest against the wind, not with it." – Winston Churchill

**PATIENCE:** "Many of life's failures are experienced by people who did not realize how close they were to success when they gave up." – Thomas Edison

**GOALS:** "You must keep your mind on the objective, not on the obstacle." – William Randolph Hearst

**DISCOVER:** "The only way to discover the limits of the possible is to go beyond them into the impossible." – Arthur C. Clark

**CONTROL:** "If you have everything under control, you're not moving fast enough." – Mario Andretti

**SEEK:** "The cave you fear to enter holds the treasures you seek." – Joseph Campbell

**LEAP:** "First you jump off the cliff, then you build wings on the way down." – Ray Bradbury

**DESTINATION:** "There are no shortcuts to any place worth going." – Beverly Sills

**DISCIPLINE:** "Seek freedom and become captive of your desires. Seek discipline and find your liberty." – Frank Herbert

**TRIUMPH:** "Success is to be measured not so much by the position that one has reached in life as by the obstacles which he has overcome." – Booker T. Washington

**UNITY:** "Many of us are more capable than some of us, but none of us is as capable as all of us." – Tom Wilson

**OVERCOME:** "No man can climb out beyond the limitations of his own character." – John Morley

These are some of my favorite quotes. You might find some you like or a favorite one that keeps you going throughout the day.

Quotes from Dr. Jim Jackson's daily devotional I'm reading:

"Peace of mind is positively the greatest gift life has to offer. And, it comes only from one place – you guessed it! From the One who made you. There is absolutely nothing else in the world of equal value to inner peace. If you have peace of mind, it does not matter how unpleasant your circumstances are. You are okay."

Good stuff!!

# CHAPTER 50
# THE END OF THE ROAD?

No way! Just a new flavor of life. Like ice cream. Ice cream has lots and lots of different flavors, and each flavor is just a different chapter of my life. Some are delicious, and some not so much. Keep that inner peace and you'll be ok. I have no idea when my last day on earth will be. If I had a terminal illness, I would have a better idea. But even then, if God says it's not your time to go, well, you won't. It's May 29, 2020. The coronavirus is still in focus. Still, people are dying, still, people getting sick. SPOILER ALERT! I have to talk about my teenage son who will be 20 on June 17th. Teenagers are a breed all their own. And it's funny how they all act basically the same. On the phone, want to sleep until noon, watching Netflix or Hulu, on the computer, and snack a lot! it has taken some adjusting to get used to this. I can be very sensitive and emotional, and get my feelings hurt easily. Hunter minds me and is a good kid, but sometimes he can really hurt my feelings. I tell him how I feel and I struggle how to handle it; but with prayer, I eventually get through it. I don't understand some teens and this electronic age we're in. He doesn't have a lot to do at home, and you can barely walk into his room. Thank goodness I only have one kid. I'm just too sensitive overall. I have to accept the new generation because they will have to accept the next one, and so on and so forth. The times are changing fast. It's Sunday, then it will be Sunday again in no time. Time flies by and the years like crashing waves coming again and again at remarkable speed. Before you know it, five years have gone by.

I do feel sorry for all the 2020 graduates who won't have a ceremony until maybe July or August. What a bummer that must be. It would be for me if I was graduating high school like my niece Sarah, and my stepdaughter Katherine from college. But they'll all make it through. They have no choice. It's the new normal! God knows how long we'll have to wear face masks. Makeup sales went down very low. If you're home most of the time, why wear makeup? Really only your family sees you. I haven't put on makeup in like two or three months. And when I did, it was to go to church mainly. I'm glad I don't wear much makeup anymore. It is freeing, I'll have you know. For me, anyway. And in the summer, it just melts right off. Then I use a bandana to absorb the sweat. So, it's useless. Not for everyone, though. I do like to wear makeup and get dressed up really pretty but haven't been able to do that lately. Chapelwood (our church) hopefully will reopen sometime in June. Hopefully!

We need not be afraid for God will turn this around for good. I'm no longer a slave to fear. I am a child of God.

# CHAPTER 51
# RECIPE FOR HAPPINESS AND REALITY

THIS IS NOT from the Bible, just a picture I bought a long time ago. I'd like to share it. No author listed.

Ingredients:

1 bag of smiles

2 cups of sharing

2 lbs. of positivity

½ cup of good humor

1 cup of self-esteem

2 spoonsful of simplicity

1 dash of goodwill

4 drops of easy-going

And 1 packet of life-loving!

Isn't that cute?! I'm making a big pot of it so I can have some every day. But truly…all that would make you happy. How could it not?!

'The most effective way to receive Jesus' peace is to let His light soak into your mind and heart until you are aglow with His very being." by Sarah Young from her book *Jesus Calling*.

[to music]:

*"You say I am loved*

*When I can't feel a thing*

*You say I am strong*

*When I think I am weak*

*And I believe, I believe. What you say of me, I believe I am yours."* – from the song "*You Say*" by Lauren Daigle.

Regarding reality on the streets now. As I said, my husband Michael is an UberEats driver, and he really does drive all over town. He's gotten on Facebook a few times and texts about the homeless. There are so many of them. More than I knew. Right here in Houston, not just other states. Setting up tents under freeways and along streets. I don't think anybody really knows how to handle it; there are too many of them. Worse in other cities. The homeless shelters are overcrowded, but some people refuse to go to a shelter. It is because they don't want to follow rules or something, or maybe they're just too full.

Michael said he's seen a lot of elderly people, too. How are they supposed to live? Can you imagine trying to eat, keep clean, use the restroom? What do you use for a restroom? Do you have toilet paper? If not, what do you use? Having clean clothes, clean underwear, clean everything! If Katherine hadn't paid our rent three different times, the church helping us, and other social services, I don't know where we'd be. I admit I was worried about if we would have to move, and then to where. "Thank you Lord God for providing for me and Michael, and letting us be able to stay in our apartment. And you are continuing to provide for us still and always will as long as we have faith and hope. Thank you so much. Amen."

It's hard not to worry (remember, it's an insult to God). So socially acceptable…isn't that crazy?! Like you have to accept it or you're not normal. What's normal anyway? Everybody has their own meaning. What's this world coming to? An end, that's what. When Jesus comes again, there will be a new world. Fear is fight or flight, and anxiety is doom and gloom. I'd rather have neither. This world can be scary. *"God's a way maker, miracle worker, promise keeper, light in the darkness."* – from the song *"Way Maker"* by Leeland. He's a lighthouse for the sailors to see. He's all those things. You just have to believe it!!

The George Floyd murder happened while writing this. So very sad. For that cop to keep his knee on that man's neck and choke him to death on TV for everyone to see. Why does human life seem so small to some? That cop murdered George Floyd in broad daylight on video from people's phones. Lots of witnesses. With cops standing around in case anybody intervened. The cop who murdered George Floyd needs to get 1st-degree murder, not 2nd or 3rd. There are good cops and bad cops. There are good people and bad people. These were bad cops. All of them should go to prison. There were riots, protests, and looting involved. Destroying stores, people's businesses. What does that solve? People are so angry! They tear up their own town. Such anger and hatred. It was all over the news for days. He left behind a wife and four kids. His young daughter said, "My daddy changed the world." They tried having peaceful protests, but I think that was all a show. Man will always fight man. How can there be peace in a world that's so corrupt? But come to the end of time, when Jesus comes again, Christianity will be seen and heard all around the world through TBN and CBN. We are reaching very remote areas of the world. Everyone will know Jesus because HE'S ALIVE! And we're getting closer to that day peace and forgiveness place in their hearts of his family. The forgiveness part will be very, very hard. He did change the world. On this earth, we will have problems, but you need not lose sight of Jesus.

# CHAPTER 52
# SARAH GRACE

ANOTHER 2020 GRADUATE in our family is my sweet and beautiful niece Sarah. Steve and Anna had her and she's their only girl. Hunter grew up with her when living with them. The cute cousins looked like brother and sister. They're about a year and a half apart and get along well.

All the 2020 graduates will never forget this year because of the coronavirus and the George Floyd murder. *"I'll never know how much it cost to see my sin upon that cross."*– I can't recall the name of the artist. Wow, all that's happened in just half a year. If I was a graduate this year, I tell you it would make a huge impact on me. Will be remembered for two horrible events that happened in 2020. I'm glad Hunter graduated last year. How very sad. My dear niece won't have all the good memories of her 2020 graduation, unfortunately.

But the graduation itself will be postponed until I think July or August. They'll have one, but it won't be the same. Having to sit six feet apart, wearing face masks. Is this really the new normal now? Their faces covered with a mask? For how long? No one knows but God, and He will get us through this pandemic. When is the question.

Sarah is a dancer, artist, and musician (violin and cello) performing in orchestra concerts. She is so sweet and nice. Very mature for her age. Knows three languages and never made below an "A" in school! Sarah will be attending the University of Texas at Austin in the Plan II Honors Program and The McCombs Business School. Whew, that's a lot! And the cool thing about it is she'll be Hunter's neighbor. He's at Southwestern in Georgetown, about half an hour from Austin. I think that is so neat!

I'm glad they'll be close by each other. Hunter has a stepbrother who lives in Austin. Michael raised his two stepchildren, Mark and Jessica, along with his own four kids. Mark lives in Austin. He's in his early 30's and is an engineer. Sarah and Hunter could go visit him. And I hear they jam!

# CHAPTER 53
# LAST BUT NOT LEAST

I WANT TO INTRODUCE Hunter's real father – his name is Donald M. White. And he hasn't seen his own son since Hunter was three months old. Yes, that's right. And Hunter will have turned 20 on June 17th. Sometimes his birthday falls on Father's Day. That was kinda ironic since Donald was never around on that day either. It's kind of a weird story, so here goes –

As I mentioned earlier in the book, I met Don through AA. He was tall, tan, silver-grey hair, and good looking. We became boyfriend and girlfriend in a short amount of time. I wrote a lot about Don in a previous chapter. But so many emotions and feelings were wrapped around that whole situation, I have to write more. It's been on my mind for 20 years. Did I do something so terribly wrong by not marrying him? I pondered on that one for a long time. When Don asked me to marry him, I said yes – in this surfside-type restaurant at Edwards Theater. It was really popular, but it's not there anymore. That was a long time ago. Edwards' big strip center is still there. Stores and restaurants have changed names, but Edwards Cinema is still there. Amy Lynn, my sister, teaches group exercise classes at LA Fitness there.

Anyway, getting off the subject. I did not want to marry Donald White when I found out he was doing heroin in my apartment while

I was staying at Steve's. Remember why? I was afraid. I didn't want to be married to a much-too-skinny heroin addict to help raise our baby. "But don't you believe in second chances, Stephanie" as I talk to myself, which is a lot. Yes, I do. Even more so now. I could have married Donald. He could have gotten in rehab again, conquered the heroin use, and we could have lived happily ever after. Could that have happened? Maybe. I'll never know. Hunter's life would have taken such a different route. First of all, he would know his half-sister and all his aunts, uncles, grandmother, and grandfather. Donald might have gotten remarried and had more kids. I don't know. Maybe I hurt Don really bad for changing my mind and telling his sister I wouldn't marry him. I used to think Don just told everyone it wasn't his kid to get back at me. Whatever happened, not one relative in Don's family has ever seen him or tried to contact me to see Hunter. That's so sad. Why not one person? I don't' know what all Don told them, but it kept everyone away – for 20 years now! It just blows my mind…20 years!!

When Hunter was a baby, I remember going to the courthouse for custody of Hunter. Donald was supposed to show up, but he didn't so I got full custody. Don knows Hunter is his son. He had to pay child support throughout Hunter's schooling. He knows beyond a shadow of a doubt Hunter is his son. And you'd think maybe someone in his family would want to know for sure, be curious or something. But nothing. Not one word, not even a whisper to want to find out for sure and see him. Hunter was an adorable blonde-haired, blue-eyed (which he got from his dad) precious baby. They all missed out on his growing up. I'm so glad Steve took Hunter from me that fateful night when I was drinking. I didn't stay sober either when Hunter was growing up. I'm an alcoholic and was a drug addict, too.

Would Donald White ever forgive me for not marrying him? No telling what our lives may have been like. But I'll never know now. I wonder if Don thinks of these things. It just makes me cry knowing what I know now and not knowing back then. Not maybe doing the right thing after all, and the tremendous shift in Hunter's life. Don wasn't there for Hunter, and I wasn't either when I was drinking. He was raised by his aunt and uncle. So, why couldn't I give Donald a second chance like I would have wanted? I don't know. I was afraid to do the wrong thing, which maybe I did. I pray Don forgives me for not marrying him. And I pray someday he'll ask for forgiveness for not being there for Hunter.

But Hunter is a good boy (a good young man, now). I'm so proud of my boy. I do have one prayer that I hope God will answer – that Hunter can meet his dad before he passes. He didn't die back then and God gave him a second chance to live again. I don't remember how old Don is, but I think I'm older, not by much. Oh, I want him to see the good man his son turned out to be. A beautiful person. He's going to college again in the fall and learning a career. "Don, I have so much to tell you about your son," I would say to him. "You would be so proud of him too!"

I want Hunter to meet his dad before he passes. I hope Hunter can forgive, too. I hope they get to meet each other, maybe get to know each other. You never know, and prayers are answered. I pray that this will happen, in Jesus' name. Amen. I hope it's meant to be. Maybe I shouldn't try to find his dad, maybe it would be bad. I just want the truth to come out. What did Donald tell his family about his own son? That not one person in his family wanted to see him. Ever! Not one person! What did Don tell his family to make this so? That's all I can think of…that he told them Hunter wasn't his son. Then why did I get child support all those years? Something's just not right. And I want to know the truth from him. I tried looking him up but his picture did not come up. I know he's alive (I think) and lives in Texas. I think close by. Please help me, Lord God, figure this out. Hunter will be 20 years old. He's a man now. He needs to know. Hunter says he doesn't care and doesn't want to know. Should I leave it alone? And if it's meant to be, it will happen? I should not worry about it anymore. As Hunter gets older, let him do what he wants when he knows what he wants.

Today, I am a beautiful creation of broken pieces, mended by God's love and grace.

I think this finds me at the end of my story for this book. I will write more later, at another time. The reason for writing this book is I hope it helps somebody…that they can relate to it with what they might be going through. It has also helped me rub some scabs off with scars remaining to remind me, but know I am healed by our mighty great God, who is the ultimate great healer. Thank you Jesus for being by my side and helping me write this book. Till next time, God bless all.

Jesus is for everyone. He belongs to the whole world. Reach out for him today!

Jesus is Lord.

Sincerely,

Stephanie Stephens-Zellner

www.ingramcontent.com/pod-product-compliance
Lightning Source LLC
Chambersburg PA
CBHW061734050726
47598CB00002B/477